U.S. Department of
Transportation

**Federal Railroad
Administration**

Cognitive and Collaborative Demands of Freight Conductor Activities: Results and Implications of a Cognitive Task Analysis

Office of Railroad
Policy and Development
Washington, DC 20590

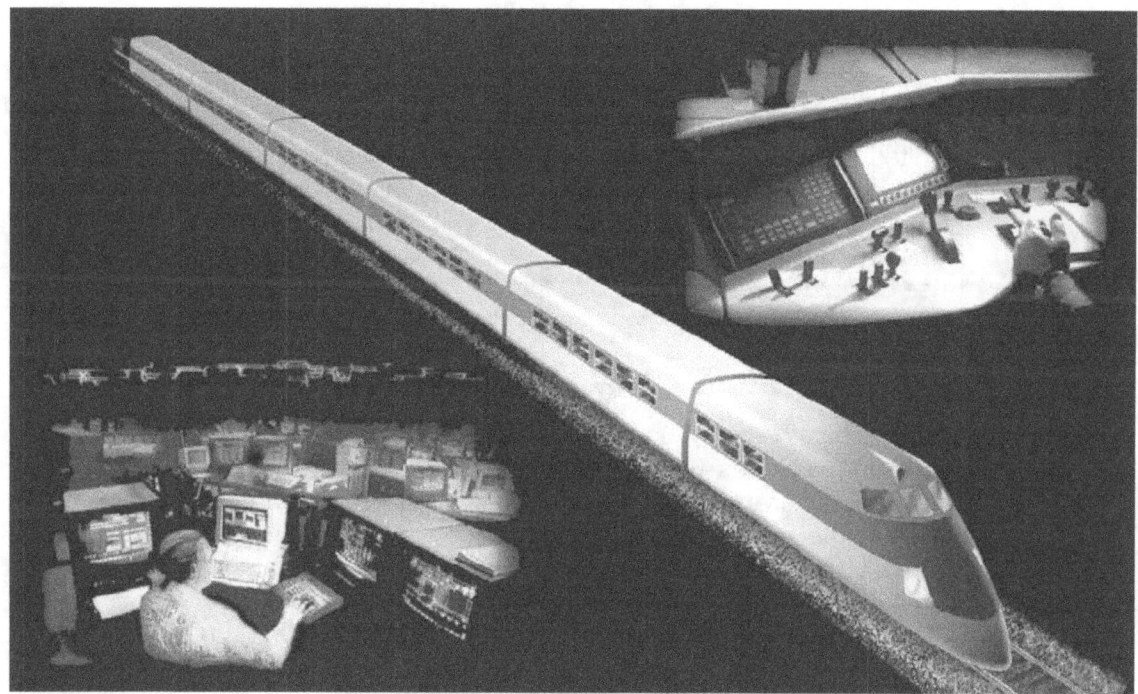

Human Factors in Railroad Operations

DOT/FRA/ORD-12/13

Final Report
July 2012

1. AGENCY USE ONLY (*LEAVE BLANK*)	2. REPORT DATE July 2012	3. REPORT TYPE AND DATES COVERED February 2009–March 2011	
4. TITLE AND SUBTITLE Cognitive and Collaborative Demands of Freight Conductor Activities: Results and Implications of a Cognitive Task Analysis			5. FUNDING NUMBERS RR04A4/JT278
6. AUTHOR(S) Hadar Rosenhand, Emilie Roth, and Jordan Multer			
7. PERFORMING ORGANIZATION NAME(S) AND ADDRESS(ES) U.S. Department of Transportation Research and Special Programs Administration John A. Volpe National Transportation systems Center Cambridge, MA 02142-1093			8. PERFORMING ORGANIZATION DOT-VNTSC-FRA-99-X
9. SPONSORING/MONITORING AGENCY NAME(S) AND ADDRESS(ES) U.S. Department of Transportation Federal Railroad Administration Office of Railroad Policy and Development Washington, DC 20590			10. SPONSORING/MONITORING AGENCY REPORT NUMBER DOT/FRA/ORD – 12/13
11. SUPPLEMENTARY NOTES Program Manager: Thomas Raslear			
12a. DISTRIBUTION/AVAILABILITY STATEMENT This document is available to the public through the FRA Web site at http://www.fra.dot.gov.			12b. DISTRIBUTION CODE

13. ABSTRACT (Maximum 200 words)

This report presents the results of a cognitive task analysis (CTA) that examined the cognitive and collaborative demands placed on conductors, as well as the knowledge and skills that experienced conductors have developed that enable them to operate trains safely and efficiently. A secondary aim of the CTA was to understand the implications of the Rail Safety Improvement Act (RSIA) of 2008 regarding the role of the freight conductor, specifically the mandate for conductor certification and implementation of positive train control (PTC). Data was collected through a combination of field observations, phone interviews, and onsite focus group sessions with experienced conductors, locomotive engineers, trainers, and training managers. A primary finding is that conductors and locomotive engineers operate as a joint cognitive system (Woods and Hollnagel, 2006). They not only work together to monitor the operating environment outside the locomotive, they also collaborate in planning activities, problem solving, and identifying and mitigating potential risk. Although the present CTA does not directly address the issue of how new technologies, such as PTC, are likely to impact the role of conductors in the future, the CTA results do identify multiple ways in which conductors contribute to safe and efficient train operation. As new PTC technologies are introduced, it will be important to assess their impact on the various functions conductors perform in support of safe and efficient train operation, as specified in this report. The CTA also uncovered a variety of knowledge and skills that distinguish experienced conductors from less experienced ones. These findings suggest an opportunity to potentially accelerate building conductor expertise through more systematic training opportunities (both on the job and in locomotive cab simulators). The report concludes with open questions and future research needs as yet uncovered by the CTA.

14. SUBJECT TERMS Cognitive task analysis, CTA, freight rail, freight conductor, conductor training, Rail Safety Improvement Act, RSIA, positive train control, PTC, conductor certification			15. NUMBER OF PAGES 72
			16. PRICE CODE
17. SECURITY CLASSIFICATION OF REPORT Unclassified	18. SECURITY CLASSIFICATION OF THIS PAGE Unclassified	19. SECURITY CLASSIFICATION OF ABSTRACT Unclassified	LIMITATION OF ABSTRACT Unclassified

METRIC/ENGLISH CONVERSION FACTORS

ENGLISH TO METRIC

LENGTH (APPROXIMATE)
1 inch (in)	=	2.5 centimeters (cm)
1 foot (ft)	=	30 centimeters (cm)
1 yard (yd)	=	0.9 meter (m)
1 mile (mi)	=	1.6 kilometers (km)

AREA (APPROXIMATE)
1 square inch (sq in, in^2)	=	6.5 square centimeters (cm^2)
1 square foot (sq ft, ft^2)	=	0.09 square meter (m^2)
1 square yard (sq yd, yd^2)	=	0.8 square meter (m^2)
1 square mile (sq mi, mi^2)	=	2.6 square kilometers (km^2)
1 acre = 0.4 hectare (he)	=	4,000 square meters (m^2)

MASS - WEIGHT (APPROXIMATE)
1 ounce (oz)	=	28 grams (gm)
1 pound (lb)	=	0.45 kilogram (kg)
1 short ton = 2,000 pounds (lb)	=	0.9 tonne (t)

VOLUME (APPROXIMATE)
1 teaspoon (tsp)	=	5 milliliters (ml)
1 tablespoon (tbsp)	=	15 milliliters (ml)
1 fluid ounce (fl oz)	=	30 milliliters (ml)
1 cup (c)	=	0.24 liter (l)
1 pint (pt)	=	0.47 liter (l)
1 quart (qt)	=	0.96 liter (l)
1 gallon (gal)	=	3.8 liters (l)
1 cubic foot (cu ft, ft^3)	=	0.03 cubic meter (m^3)
1 cubic yard (cu yd, yd^3)	=	0.76 cubic meter (m^3)

TEMPERATURE (EXACT)
$[(x-32)(5/9)]$ °F $=$ y °C

METRIC TO ENGLISH

LENGTH (APPROXIMATE)
1 millimeter (mm)	=	0.04 inch (in)
1 centimeter (cm)	=	0.4 inch (in)
1 meter (m)	=	3.3 feet (ft)
1 meter (m)	=	1.1 yards (yd)
1 kilometer (km)	=	0.6 mile (mi)

AREA (APPROXIMATE)
1 square centimeter (cm^2)	=	0.16 square inch (sq in, in^2)
1 square meter (m^2)	=	1.2 square yards (sq yd, yd^2)
1 square kilometer (km^2)	=	0.4 square mile (sq mi, mi^2)
10,000 square meters (m^2)	=	1 hectare (ha) = 2.5 acres

MASS - WEIGHT (APPROXIMATE)
1 gram (gm)	=	0.036 ounce (oz)
1 kilogram (kg)	=	2.2 pounds (lb)
1 tonne (t)	=	1,000 kilograms (kg)
	=	1.1 short tons

VOLUME (APPROXIMATE)
1 milliliter (ml)	=	0.03 fluid ounce (fl oz)
1 liter (l)	=	2.1 pints (pt)
1 liter (l)	=	1.06 quarts (qt)
1 liter (l)	=	0.26 gallon (gal)
1 cubic meter (m^3)	=	36 cubic feet (cu ft, ft^3)
1 cubic meter (m^3)	=	1.3 cubic yards (cu yd, yd^3)

TEMPERATURE (EXACT)
$[(9/5) y + 32]$ °C $=$ x °F

QUICK INCH - CENTIMETER LENGTH CONVERSION

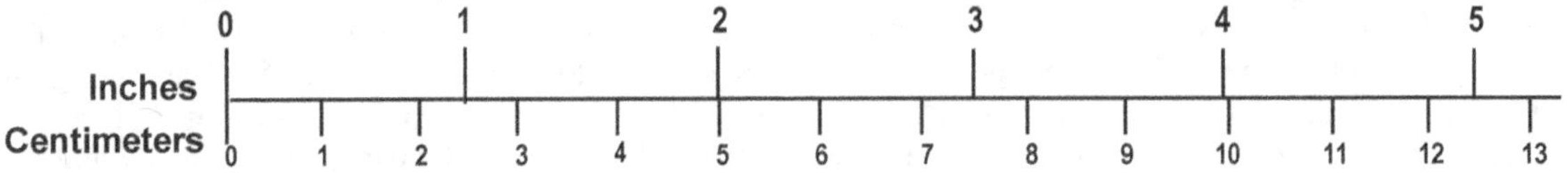

QUICK FAHRENHEIT - CELSIUS TEMPERATURE CONVERSIO

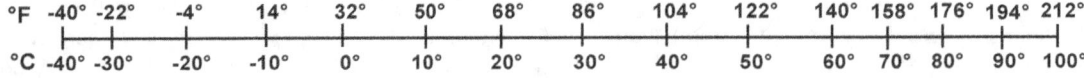

°F	-40°	-22°	-4°	14°	32°	50°	68°	86°	104°	122°	140°	158°	176°	194°	212°
°C	-40°	-30°	-20°	-10°	0°	10°	20°	30°	40°	50°	60°	70°	80°	90°	100°

For more exact and or other conversion factors, see NIST Miscellaneous Publication 286, Units of Weights and Measures. Price $2.50
SD Catalog No. C13 10286
Updated 6/17/98

Acknowledgments

The Federal Railroad Administration's (FRA) Office of Research and Development funded this research effort. We thank the Office of Research and Development, and Dr. Thomas Raslear, in particular, for the opportunity to perform and document cognitive analyses of train crews.

Many people and organizations made the completion of this task possible. We thank Nacho Quintero, Senior Manager of Conductor Training, and the National Academy of Railroad Sciences (NARS) for providing us with the opportunity to interview conductor training instructors and for facilitating our visit to the NARS training facility. We also thank Larry Breedon, General Manager, Operating Practices, and Union Pacific Railroad for providing us with the opportunity to interview conductors, engineers, conductor trainers and managers, and total safety culture employees at Union Pacific Railroad. We give special thanks to James Robinson, Regional Director of the Southern Region, Union Pacific Railroad, for making the trip to the Beaumont and Houston Yards so successful, and facilitating the many focus groups and yard visits. We also thank Michael Sanders, Deputy Region 8 Administrator, FRA, for providing us with the opportunity to interview conductors working in mountain grade territory. We thank James Stem of the United Transportation Union, Jeff Moller of the Association of American Railroads, Bill Moore-Ede of the Transportation Technology Center, Inc., John Grundman, former assistant Vice President of Safety for BNSF Railway, and John Conklin and Mike Jones of FRA for sharing their knowledge and insight with us. We also acknowledge Ben Walsh and his Job Analysis team at the University of Connecticut, with whom we collaborated and shared information.

Finally, we want to express our special thanks to all of the locomotive engineers, conductors, and trainers who agreed to participate in the interviews and focus groups. Their candid comments and insights were critical to the success of this project.

Contents

Tables

Executive Summary

Railroad operations in the United States are undergoing rapid changes. These changes are due in part to the Rail Safety Improvement Act of 2008 (RSIA), which calls for, among other things, enhancements in railroad conductor certification programs and the implementation of positive train control (PTC) on applicable freight and passenger rail lines. As part of its ongoing efforts to investigate the safety implications of emerging technologies on railroad operations, the Federal Railroad Administration's (FRA) Office of Research and Development sponsored a series of cognitive task analyses (CTA) to examine the cognitive and collaborative demands associated with different railroad operations. The first CTA focused on railroad dispatchers (Roth, Malsch, and Multer, 2001). A second CTA addressed roadway worker activities (Roth and Multer, 2007). The third CTA focused on locomotive engineers (Roth and Multer, 2009). The present report documents the results of a CTA that was conducted to examine the cognitive and collaborative activities of the freight train conductor.

Study Objectives and Method

The purpose of the freight train conductor CTA was to gain an understanding of the role of conductors in today's freight rail operations. To do this, researchers sought to understand the cognitive and collaborative activities associated with the role of the conductor, the situational factors that arise to complicate performance, and the knowledge and skills that experienced freight train conductors have developed to cope with performance demands so as to maintain a safe and efficient operation. A related aim was to understand the implications of RSIA on the role of the conductor, specifically the mandate for conductor certification and implementation of PTC. The goal was to understand current conductor training programs, to provide insight to FRA for the conductor certification effort, and, to the extent possible, to understand and anticipate potential impacts of PTC implementation on the conductor's work and future training trends.

The report focuses primarily on freight train conductors operating on the mainline. Mainline freight train crews operating in the United States generally include a locomotive engineer and a conductor. Our findings indicate that the conductor and the locomotive engineer function as an integrated team that often operate as a single unit with a common goal. As such, the cognitive and collaborative challenges and skills documented in the locomotive engineer CTA largely apply to conductors. Similarly, the results documented here will also generally apply to the locomotive engineer.

The CTA was based on several sets of interviews and site visits conducted between January 2009 and April 2010. Interviews and focus groups were conducted with stakeholders and railroad practitioners, experienced conductors, and conductor trainers and training managers, including representatives from FRA, American Association of Railroads (AAR), United Transportation Union (UTU), Transportation Technology Center, Inc. (TTCI), National Academy of Railroad Sciences (NARS), BNSF Railway (BNSF), and Union Pacific Railroad (UP). Site visits included a trip to the NARS facility in the UP Beaumont Yard and the UP Houston Yard.

Results

Cognitive Tasks and Associated Challenges

A conductor is defined as the crewmember in charge of a train or yard crew. Freight conductors supervise pre-trip activities, over-the-road operation, and post-trip activities to ensure overall safe and efficient train movement.

To better understand the cognitive tasks and challenges associated with the freight conductor's job, we broke the job duties down into five categories:

- Managing the train consist
- Coordinating with the locomotive engineer for safe and efficient en route operation
- Interacting with dispatchers/roadway workers and others outside the locomotive cab
- Dealing with exceptional situations (e.g., diagnosing and responding to train problems)
- Managing paperwork

The conductor's role in managing the train consist means that he or she must understand train makeup rules and apply them both in the yard and on the mainline. Experienced conductors understand the implications of car placement, car consist, and car weight and shape when building trains. Conductors on the mainline must look over the train consist and car list prior to departing the yard to ensure proper train makeup. Conductors must understand how the train's consist will affect train handling, which is important to ensure locomotive engineer compliance when operating the train.

En route, one of the conductor's main tasks is supervising overall operation and administration of the train to ensure safe and efficient operation. This involves communicating and coordinating closely with the locomotive engineer, monitoring locomotive engineer performance, and providing backup as needed. Conductors handle all radio communication and take care of paperwork when the train is in motion so that the locomotive engineer can concentrate on operating the train. The conductor also serves to remind the engineer about upcoming signals and slow orders and provides "look ahead" information to alert the engineer to hills, curves, grade crossings, etc. If the locomotive engineer is not in compliance with the railroad's operating rules, it is the conductor's job to bring it to the locomotive engineer's attention or pull the emergency brake to bring the train to an emergency stop if he or she feels the train, its crew, or others outside the train are in danger. Finally, the conductor's presence in the cab may help to keep the locomotive engineer awake and alert, and vice versa (Frings, 2011).

The conductor is also in charge of all radio communications in the cab. Radio communications come in spurts, meaning there can be lulls in communication and times of heavy interaction that require conductors to multitask. For example, a conductor may need to communicate with the dispatcher (or a roadway worker), copy the information back to the dispatcher and write it down, make sure the engineer received the information, and also maintain awareness of conditions outside the cab, which includes calling out signals and speed restrictions. This can be especially challenging when the dispatcher is speaking quickly and using railroad jargon.

Unexpected situations include anything from train equipment issues (e.g., mechanical performance, operability, etc.), to collisions and derailments. Although these unanticipated events run the gamut, train equipment issues are perhaps the most common unanticipated events that arise en route, and in these cases, it is the conductor who is responsible for troubleshooting and, when possible, repairing the problem.

Finally, conductors are required to fill out and maintain all paperwork for the train, including track warrants, work orders, train consist, etc. At the start of a shift, the conductor's duty is to gather all the paperwork and make two copies, one for him/herself and one for the engineer, look it over, and check for errors. In addition to maintaining paperwork relating to the trip, the conductor must also be vigilant about keeping the railroad's rulebook up to date, which can be challenging because of the frequency with which operating rules are updated. Finally, while en route, the conductor is responsible for documenting the trip in a log. This includes writing down slow orders and authorizations from the dispatcher and recording signal indications as they are passed as well as filling out other forms as necessary.

Challenges Associated with Mountain Grade Territory

A significant finding of the CTA was that operating territory can affect the complexity of the conductor's job to a great degree. Specifically, operating in mountain grade territory adds complexity to the job and introduces additional cognitive demands on both the conductor and the locomotive engineer.

Overarching Cognitive Challenges

Interviews with conductors and trainers indicate that it can take up to 5 years to gain sufficient experience to become a confident, expert conductor. We sought to understand the type of knowledge and cognitive skills that conductors develop over time, largely acquired through on-the-job experience, that enable them to function safely and efficiently. The following points summarize our findings of the characteristics that differentiate expert conductors from less experienced ones.

- Knowledge of the Territory - Knowledge of the territory, including a detailed mental model of the physical landscape in which they operate, is critical to enabling train crews to operate efficiently as well as to anticipate and mitigate risks to themselves and others.

- Ability to Maintain Situation Awareness of Surroundings - Conductors need to be continuously aware of their physical surroundings, whether they are in the locomotive, switching cars on the ground, or walking to and from the train. They need to maintain awareness of the location of other trains and machines on adjacent tracks, the location of cars and whether they are properly secured, and the location of people working on or about the track.

- Ability to Project Effect of Consist on Train Dynamics - The ability to successfully estimate the impact of consist characteristics (e.g., number of cars, length, and weight) on train dynamics is another characteristic conductors develop over time. Although operating the train is the responsibility of the locomotive engineer, the conductor also needs to develop an understanding of the impact of consist characteristics on train dynamics to function in his or her general role of supervising train operations. An understanding of how the consist can impact train dynamics is needed to enable conductors to effectively monitor the performance of the locomotive engineer and provide backup support as needed.

- Ability to Problem Solve - Conductors are routinely confronted with novel situations for which they have to perform mental simulations to identify a correct solution. Building trains and car placement issues, for example, often require problem solving and mental simulation, as do unanticipated, emergency situations.

- <u>Ability to Plan Ahead</u> - Conductors need to project into the future to anticipate and prepare for what is coming up next on the road (e.g., signals, curves, grade crossings, and train meets). It is also important to think ahead about various tasks they will need to accomplish over the shift so as to plan the most efficient way to accomplish them.

- <u>Ability to Multitask</u> - Another skill that differentiates more experienced from less experienced conductors is the ability to manage multiple demands on their attention. Experienced conductors have learned strategies for managing and prioritizing these competing demands.

- <u>Ability to Exploit External Memory Aids</u> - Mainline operations place heavy demands on memory. Experienced conductors have developed a variety of strategies that rely on external aids to support memory, including strategies to support prospective memory that allow themselves to focus their attention on the task at hand.

- <u>Ability to Foster Shared Situation Awareness through Active Communication</u> - Conductors need to be able to communicate effectively with the locomotive engineer as well as other members of the train crew to maintain shared situational awareness, facilitate efficient work, and enhance safety. This communication needs to be an active, ongoing process, beginning with an initial job briefing and continuing en route through active communication such as calling out signals and confirming that the locomotive engineer acknowledged them.

In addition to learning about the types of knowledge and skills that enable experienced conductors to perform more effectively, the CTA also uncovered effects of lack of experience on conductor performance. Less experienced conductors, we found, are less able to handle situations that require balancing multiple demands on attention, and they are less able to effectively problem-solve, plan ahead, or identify and avoid potential hazards. Because they have had less "first-hand" experience on the job, they are typically less confident in their knowledge and ability.

Training

The CTA sought to assess current training practices and trends to help identify future training needs. Currently, there is no conductor training standard or uniform syllabus among railroads and conductor training programs, though they generally include a mixture of classroom and on-the-job training (OJT). The length of each training program varies by railroad. We found that different railroads have different training models, and the industry is experiencing different training trends among the various railroads. For example, many railroads have been implementing crew resource management (CRM) training, which focuses on training the crew to function optimally as a team. Our findings point to a need for a more uniform standard of training. Many conductors expressed a desire to standardize OJT so that guidelines exist for situations and events all conductor trainees must experience in training. Conductors specifically indicated the need to train for rare but serious events and incidents, and stressed the importance of training so that tasks become intuitive and reflexive (perhaps more so in mountain grade territory). Finally, conductors mentioned the need to train new hires to anticipate and discuss risk, and noted that CRM training is especially important in giving new hires the confidence to speak candidly with experienced engineers about risks.

Key Findings

Locomotive Engineer and Conductor Function As a Joint Cognitive System

From interviews with conductors and locomotive engineers during the Conductor CTA and the earlier Locomotive Engineer CTA (Roth and Multer, 2007) it is clear that both employees function as a joint cognitive system (Woods and Hollnagel, 2006). They closely coordinate tasks with each other, adaptively share perceptual and cognitive load, and rely on each other to successfully accomplish the mission of the train. The conductor and locomotive engineer not only serve as an extension of "eyes" and "ears" for each other, catching and communicating information that the other may have missed, but they also extend each other cognitively—filling in knowledge gaps, providing reminders for upcoming tasks, and contributing jointly to problem-solving and decisionmaking situations that arise. This is especially true when a less experienced crewmember is paired with a more experienced crewmember.

The Role of Conductors in Handling Unanticipated Situations

Another important role that conductors play on the mainline is handling unanticipated situations. This includes a variety of situations where conductors need to troubleshoot the source of the problem and take appropriate action. These unanticipated situations impose cognitive as well as physical demands on the conductor. Experienced conductors have developed a variety of skills and strategies that enable them to handle these non-routine situations more safely and efficiently. This knowledge is primarily gained in the field through first-hand on-the-job experience as well as by working with more experienced conductors and engineers.

Implications of Results

The Role of Conductors and PTC Technology

One of the questions that motivated the cognitive task analysis was how new technologies, such as PTC, are likely to impact the role of conductors in the future. The cognitive task analysis addresses this issue by laying out the multiple ways in which conductors contribute to safe and efficient train operations and contrasts this with the anticipated features of PTC systems.

Findings from the CTA indicate that PTC will not account for all of the cognitive support functions the conductor currently provides. For example, conductors support locomotive engineers in monitoring conditions outside the cab for potential obstacles and hazards that are undetected by automated systems, filling knowledge gaps that locomotive engineers may have, and supporting decisionmaking (e.g., where to stop to avoid blocking a grade crossing). Conductors also serve an important role in handling unanticipated events as well as keeping the locomotive engineer alert, especially on long monotonous trips where there is a risk of falling asleep.

Potential to Accelerate Development of Expertise

The results of the CTA suggest an opportunity to potentially accelerate building conductor expertise by providing a broader set of carefully selected experiences as part of OJT. These would potentially enable new conductors to more quickly build up their knowledge of the territory and direct experience with a variety of situations.

The results also point to the importance of teaching conductors and locomotive engineers effective cab communication and job briefing skills. More focus on effective communication would enhance teamwork and encourage joint problem-solving and decisionmaking that leverages the knowledge and skills of the entire train crew for safer and more efficient performance.

Finally the results of the cognitive task analysis point to the value of carefully pairing conductors and locomotive engineers so that less experienced individuals are paired with more experienced ones. This not only makes for a safer and more efficient train crew but also it provides opportunities for knowledge transfer between crewmembers, further accelerating development of expertise.

Future Research Needs

The cognitive task analysis uncovered several open questions relating to conductor expertise, conductor training, and conductor certification. Future research is needed to answer these questions. For example, although the CTA identified the knowledge and skills required of expert conductors at a high level, additional studies can be performed to examine the cognitive skills at a more detailed level of analysis. Other promising lines for future research relate to how skills expand with level of expertise, how CRM can contribute to safer and more effective teamwork, and the impact of PTC displays on crew cognitive and collaborative processes. Many of these open questions can be explored through the use of simulator studies.

1. Introduction

As part of its efforts to investigate the safety implications of applying emerging technologies to railroad operations, FRA's Office of Research and Development, Office of Railroad Policy and Development, sponsored a series of preliminary CTAs to gain an understanding of the cognitive and collaborative demands associated with various railroad operations positions. This has included CTAs for railroad dispatchers (Roth, Malsch, and Multer, 2001), roadway worker activities (Roth and Multer, 2007), and locomotive engineers (Roth and Multer, 2007). The present report documents the results of a CTA that was conducted to examine the cognitive and collaborative activities of the freight train conductor.

Section 1 provides a general introduction to cognitive task analyses methods and information goals, the purpose and scope for this CTA, and an overview of the role and responsibilities of conductors. General conductor responsibilities were drawn from a review of railroad operating rule books, job descriptions, a conductor and brakeman task analysis published in 1974, and a job task analysis (Walsh et al., 2010). The job task analysis, which was done concurrently and in coordination with the CTA and sponsored by FRA, provided a summary of major tasks and knowledge, skills, and abilities of conductors. Section 2 describes the methodology that was used to conduct the CTA, including the stakeholder interviews and the specific railroad sites that were visited.

Section 3 presents the results of the CTA, beginning with a discussion of the locomotive engineer and conductor as a joint cognitive team and a brief overview of the work of conductors. The overarching cognitive challenges are presented and discussed in the following sections, which include a discussion of the cognitive tasks and associated challenges of the work of conductors and the overarching knowledge and cognitive skill requirements of conductors.

Section 4 summarizes the results of the CTA and their implications. This includes a discussion of the potential impact of PTC technology on the role of conductors as well as a discussion of opportunities to accelerate development of conductor expertise through systematic OJT. Finally, the report concludes with open questions the freight conductor CTA raised and related future research needs.

1.1 CTA Objectives and Approach

CTA methods have grown out of the need to explicitly identify and take into account the cognitive requirements inherent in performing complex work (Potter et al., 2000; Schraagen et al., 2000). A CTA analyzes the high-level cognitive and collaborative functions that individuals and teams need to engage in to meet the demands of the work (Klein, Klein, and Klein, 2000; Klein et al., 2003; Klein, Moon, and Hoffman, 2006; Patterson et al., 2010). Cognitive functions relevant to human performance in complex, dynamic, high-risk domains include:

- detecting/noticing
- sense-making/understanding
- directing attention
- planning/deciding
- communicating/coordinating (teamwork functions)

7

- managing workload

A variety of specific CTA techniques have been developed that draw on basic principles and methods of cognitive psychology. These include structured interview techniques; critical incident analysis methods that investigate actual incidents that have occurred in the past; and cognitive field observation studies that examine performance in actual environments or in high-fidelity simulators. A broad overview of CTA methods and applications can be found in Schraagen et al., 2000; Crandall et al., 2006; and Bisantz and Roth, 2008.

Although there are a variety of methods for performing cognitive task and work analyses, they share a common goal of providing information about two mutually reinforcing perspectives. One perspective focuses on the fundamental characteristics of the work domain and the cognitive demands they impose. The other perspective focuses on how current practitioners respond to the demands of the domain. This includes a description of the knowledge and skills practitioners have developed to operate effectively as well as any limitations in knowledge and strategies that contribute to performance problems.

CTA methods focus particularly on documenting *illustrative cases*, also referred to as *critical incidents*, which describe specific actual situations that domain practitioners have experienced. Critical incidents provide evidence for the types of cognitively challenging situations that can arise that domain practitioners need to be able to effectively handle. Critical incidents are also used to provide evidence of the types of knowledge, skills, and strategies that experienced domain practitioners have developed that allow them to cope effectively with these cognitively demanding situations. In addition, critical incidents are typically identified either through direct field observations and/or via structured interview techniques.

A particular emphasis of CTA methods is to uncover and document informal strategies that experienced domain practitioners have developed that are not captured in formal training and procedural guidance documents. These strategies often contribute substantively to safe and efficient performance and are thus valuable to document (Roth, Multer, and Scott, 2009). They can provide guidance for future training as well as clues to performance demands that are currently not well supported that can drive new human-system interface requirements.

The results of a CTA reveal:

(1) the factors that contribute to cognitive performance difficulty;

(2) the knowledge and skills expert practitioners have developed to cope with task demands; and

(3) opportunities to improve individual and team cognitive performance in a domain through new forms of training, user interfaces, or decision aids.

The freight train conductor CTA was performed based on a combination of structured interviews with stakeholders in industry, labor and government, interviews and focus groups with conductors, locomotive engineers, conductor trainers, and training managers and observations at rail yards.

1.2 Purpose of Conductor CTA

The need for a cognitive task analysis arises from the changing nature of the train crew's job over time. Since the beginning of railroad operations in the late 1800s to the present time, freight train operations have evolved dramatically. Equipment has been updated and new technologies have been implemented, to name a few of the changes. Consequently, the role of the freight conductor has evolved. It has gone from being primarily physical in nature to consisting of predominantly cognitive work.

The purpose of the freight train conductor CTA was to gain an understanding of the role of conductors in today's mainline operation. The goal was to understand the cognitive and collaborative activities associated with the role of the freight train conductor, the situational factors that arise to complicate performance, and the knowledge and skills that experienced freight train conductors have developed to cope with performance demands so as to maintain safe and efficient operation.

In October 2008, shortly after work on the freight train conductor CTA began, the Rail Safety Improvement Act of 2008 (RSIA) was enacted into law. Two conditions of RSIA in particular were taken into consideration for the CTA work: the mandates for regulation of conductor certification and for installation of PTC systems on qualifying rail lines by December 2015. PTC refers to technology designed to prevent train-to-train collisions, overspeed derailments, and injuries to roadway workers operating within their limits of authority as a result of unauthorized train incursion.

In light of conductor certification rulemaking activity under way at the time of this research, the CTA set a goal to document how current conductor training programs operate and identify future training trends. As part of this effort, we sought to understand the differences between experienced and inexperienced conductors and asked conductors to provide details about incidents or hardships they faced on the job and how they dealt with them as well as what they believe should be covered in training that currently is missing. Finally, we took CRM into consideration for possible training improvements. We sought to understand and document communication and collaboration between conductors and locomotive engineers, dispatchers, and other railroad workers (e.g., other train crews, yardmasters, and roadway workers) and how this impacts conductor performance.

Although the RSIA mandate for PTC installation did not directly impact conductors (the mandate called for train crews to continue under current operating rules, with PTC as a non-vital means to prevent railroad incidents), we sought to identify the potential impacts of this new technology on the conductor's work.

1.3 Scope and Focus of Conductor CTA

The CTA focused on freight conductors operating on the mainline. Freight rail, rather than passenger rail, was chosen because of the relatively more complex nature of the job and because freight transport accounts for the majority of rail operations in the United States. Although our focus was on freight train conductors operating on the mainline, the report also includes discussion of the conductor in yard operations.

9

To get as broad a perspective as possible, we interviewed trainers who provide general conductor training and then conducted interviews with training instructors and experienced conductors working over territory that exhibited complexity along multiple dimensions. We complemented the site visits with phone-based interviews of conductors working in mountainous territory. From these interviews, we were able to get the perspectives of freight train conductors with experience working industry and mainline jobs over flat terrain and mountain grade territory, across territories that included tracks owned by different railroads, and with varying types of cargo ranging from grain to hazardous materials.

2.   Method

Before beginning the CTA, we sought to understand the general roles and responsibilities of conductors. This knowledge was acquired by reviewing operating manuals, railroad rulebooks, various conductor job descriptions, and prior task analyses, including the CTAs for railroad dispatchers (Roth et al., 2001), roadway worker activities (Roth and Multer, 2007), and locomotive engineers (Roth and Multer, 2007).

The CTA was based on a series of interviews and site visits conducted between January 2009 and April 2010. Interviews were conducted in three parts among various stakeholders and railroad practitioners. All interviews were conducted by using a set of predefined questions that served as a "checklist" of topics to be covered. The question sets were not used as a script; therefore, actual questions asked and their order varied depending on participant responses.

Initial interviews were conducted among stakeholders, including members of industry, labor, and government, to gain a broad perspective of railroad trends and developments that are likely to impact roles and activities of conductors. In addition, these interviews were conducted to gain stakeholder perspective on emerging technologies and how they are likely to impact conductor performance and what issues, concerns, and open questions they raise. Information regarding the stakeholders and railroad practitioners may be found in Table 1. A total of six stakeholder interviews were conducted that included three industry representatives, one labor representative, and two government representatives.

Table 1. Stakeholder Interviews	
Stakeholder	**Organization**
Industry	AAR, TTCI, BNSF
Labor	UTU
Government	FRA

Topics covered during these interviews included:

- Role of conductors in different operations - freight versus passenger, mainline versus yard
- Mainline freight conductor roles and responsibilities
- Mainline freight conductor skills and abilities
- Conductor training across the industry
- Perspective on conductor certification and certification requirements
- Emerging technology, specifically PTC, and its prospective impact on the role of the conductor

See Appendix A for a set of stakeholder interview questions.

A second series of interviews focused on conductor training. The objective was to understand current conductor training programs to inform the conductor certification process.

A total of three interviews were conducted with directors of conductor training at CSX Corporation (CSX), UP, and NARS [1] training facility. Topics covered during these interviews included:

- Demographics of new hires
- Length of training
- OJT versus training in the classroom
- Testing and evaluation of new conductors
- Perspective on conductor certification

See Appendix B for the interview questions.

We conducted the third series of interviews with experienced freight train conductors, locomotive engineers who have worked as freight conductors, and conductor training instructors each with different experiences ranging from working with hazmat, on mountain grade territory, on long and short-haul freight operations, including routes that cross territories and operate over different railroad tracks under different operating rules, and in the yard (see Table 2 for a breakdown of interview types, conductor affiliations, and conductor past work experience).

Table 2. Conductor Interviews		
Railroad	**Practitioner**	**Territory Characteristics**
NARS Training Facility (Overland Park, Kansas)	4 Conductor Training Instructors	Overview
UP Beaumont Yard (Texas) UP Houston Yard (Texas)	3 Freight Conductors 3 Engineers 3 Full-Time Safety Culture Employees 2 Peer Instructors	Industrial Local Service Long Haul Hazmat Flat Terrain
BNSF (phone)	1 Freight Conductor/UTU State Legislative Director	Mountain Grade Hazmat
UP (phone)	1 Freight Conductor/UTU State Legislative Director	Mountain Grade

These interviews were done over the phone and onsite at the NARS training facility and at two different UP rail yards. Experienced conductors were asked about the knowledge and skills they acquired while on the job. The objective was to document conductor activities and practices that contribute to safe and efficient operation, and understand what differentiates experienced conductors from less experienced ones. Conductors were also asked about their perspective on the RSIA mandate for conductor certification as well as their perspective on PTC.

Interviewees were recruited through contacts with railroad management and labor union representatives. Interviews were conducted with individuals or groups of up to three people

---

[1] NARS is a national railroad training academy. NARS conductor trainees are given a broad overview of conductor training, including classroom training on all territory characteristics.

representing a single craft. One interviewer led the interview sessions while the other interviewer took notes and asked occasional follow-up questions. Interview question sets varied depending on who was being interviewed with the exception of freight conductors and locomotive engineers, who were interviewed using the same set of interview questions. However, interview question sets served as a checklist of topics only, questions asked varied according to participant responses so no two interviews were the same. See Appendix C for interview question set guidelines.

Topics covered during these interviews included:

- Conductor Cognitive Demands
  - Mental workload
  - Attention demands
  - Vigilance
  - Memory demands
- Conductor Collaborative Demands
  - Conductor as supervisory role
  - Communication with train crew
  - Handling unanticipated events/Troubleshooting
  - Safety
- Conductor Training
  - Current training practices
  - OJT
  - Perspective on conductor certification
- Emerging Technology
  - Impact of new technology on training
  - Perspective on PTC

Interviews and focus groups lasted between 1 and 2 hours and were tape-recorded, if the participant granted consent. Interviewers then transcribed and analyzed interview content with the goal of identifying recurrent themes and specific incidents described by participants that illustrated those themes.

The analysis focused on identifying the following issues:

- cognitive and collaborative demands in the current environment that contribute to performance difficulties and errors;
- types of errors that can arise, with an emphasis on errors more likely to occur among less experienced practitioners;
- skills and strategies that experienced practitioners have developed to build and maintain shared situation awareness, to avoid or catch errors, and to improve efficiency and enhance safety.

As part of the analysis, common themes relating to conductor training across the industry were extracted to address two industry concerns. These concerns included:

- an examination of current conductor training programs and opportunities to enhance and/or improve the training process, which would serve as recommendations for the conductor certification mandate; and
- themes relating to the potential impact of PTC on the role of the conductor.

3. Results and Discussion

An overview of the roles and responsibilities of conductors is presented in Section 3.1 to provide context for the CTA. Sections 3.2 through 3.8 present results from interviews and focus groups, beginning with a discussion about the locomotive engineer and conductor as a joint cognitive team. Cognitive tasks and challenges are also presented, followed by overarching knowledge and skill requirements for expert performance and effects of lack of experience on performance. Section 3.8 presents findings related to training, including current training practices, training trends, and training needs.

3.1 Overview of Roles and Responsibilities of Conductors

To understand the cognitive activities and associated challenges faced by a freight conductor, we first need to understand his/her general roles and responsibilities.

Mainline freight operations generally consist of a two-person crew, the locomotive engineer and the conductor. The locomotive engineer is responsible for operating the train. The conductor, in broad terms, is in charge of the train, including supervising train operations and train safety and efficiency. In the cab, the conductor handles all pre- and post-trip activities, including ensuring accurate train makeup, handling all radio communications, and filling out all required forms. The conductor is also responsible for providing reminders to the locomotive engineer of speed restrictions and limits of authority and ensuring compliance. This information is typically located on paperwork given to the crew prior to the start of a trip. The conductor also communicates with the dispatcher while en route to receive trip information and is in charge of writing down the information and relaying it to the locomotive engineer. The conductor's responsibilities extend beyond the cab (e.g., verifying placement of cars on the train and ensuring accurate hazmat placement, switching and setting out cars, cutting crossings, inspecting equipment, and when necessary, troubleshooting and repairing cars.

Train crews, including the conductor, work from operating rulebooks. The most commonly used railroad rulebooks are the Northeast Operating Rules Advisory Committee (NORAC) and the General Code of Operating Rules (GCOR). Some railroads have their own rulebooks, which may be customized versions of NORAC or GCOR.

GCOR, which has a larger member group than NORAC, defines conductor responsibilities to be the following:

1. *The conductor supervises the operation and administration of the train (if trains are combined with more than one conductor on board, the conductor with the most seniority takes charge). All persons employed on the train must obey the conductor's instructions, unless the instructions endanger the train's safety or violate the rules. If any doubts arise concerning the authority for proceeding or safety, the conductor must consult with the engineer who will be equally responsible for the safety and proper handling of the train.*

15

2. *The conductor must advise the engineer and train dispatcher of any restriction placed on equipment being handled.*

3. *The conductor must remind the engineer that the train is approaching an area restricted by:*

   - *Limits of authority*
   - *Track warrant*
   - *Track bulletin*
   - *Radio speed restriction*

   The conductor must inform the engineer after the train passes the last station, but at least 2 miles from the restriction.

4. *When the conductor is not present, other crew members must obey the instructions of the engineer concerning rules, safety, and protection of the train.*

5. *Freight conductors are responsible for the freight carried by their train. They are also responsible for ensuring that the freight is delivered with any accompanying documents to its destination or terminals. Freight conductors must maintain any required records.*

In understanding the tasks of the conductor, we also examined other task analyses, including a 1974 train conductor and brakeman task analysis (Sanders, Jankovich, and Goodpaster, 1974) and an FRA-sponsored job task analysis (Walsh et al., 2010) conducted by researchers at the University of Connecticut.

Using the aforementioned sources, as well as the results of our own analyses, we developed a framework for characterizing a conductor's tasks for the purposes of this CTA. We classify them into five major categories, which serve as the framework for organizing and reporting our results. These include:

- Managing the train consist
- Coordinating with the locomotive engineer for safe and efficient en route operation
- Interacting with dispatchers/roadway workers and others outside the cab
- Managing paperwork
- Dealing with exceptional situations (e.g., diagnosing and responding to mechanical problems or conditions in the operating environment)

3.2   Locomotive Engineer and Conductor Operate as a Joint Cognitive System

From interviews with conductors and locomotive engineers during the conductor CTA and the earlier locomotive engineer CTA (Roth and Multer, 2007), it is clear that the conductor and the locomotive engineer function as a joint cognitive system (Woods and Hollnagel, 2006). The phrase "joint cognitive system" is intended to emphasize that the conductor and the locomotive engineer work together as an integrated team that functions in many ways as a single unit with a common goal.

The results of the conductor CTA provided many examples illustrating how conductors and locomotive engineers function as a joint cognitive system. The examples, documented below, make clear that conductors and locomotive engineers closely coordinate tasks with one another, adaptively share perceptual and cognitive load, and rely on one another to successfully accomplish the mission of the train. The conductor and locomotive engineer not only serve as an extension of "eyes" and "ears" for each other, catching and communicating information that the other may have missed, but they also extend each other cognitively, filling in knowledge gaps, providing reminders for upcoming tasks, and contributing jointly to problem solving and decisionmaking situations that arise.

The results of the conductor CTA also made clear that to perform effectively, conductors and locomotive engineers need to engage in behaviors that have been found to be characteristic of high performing teams across industries (Salas et al.; Salas et al., 2011). This includes mutual performance monitoring and offering backup support as needed. To effectively support each other, both team members need to know enough about the other's work to anticipate needs, provide help, and intervene when necessary to prevent error. For example, as is described below, although it is the locomotive engineer who is responsible for knowing how to physically operate the train, the conductor must also understand the impact of various factors (e.g., operating restrictions due to train weight and length, upcoming crossings and slow orders) on train handling to appropriately support the locomotive engineer and ensure safe train operation.

Because conductors and locomotive engineers work as such a tightly coupled team, many of the cognitive and collaborative challenges and skills that were documented in the locomotive engineer CTA apply for the conductor as well. Similarly, the results documented here will generally also apply to the locomotive engineer.

3.3 Overview of the Work of Conductors

The conductor is responsible for specific tasks. These tasks vary depending on the type of work the conductor performs. Generally, freight conductors' work fall into one of the following three categories:

- Yard
- Local/Industry Jobs
- Long Haul Mainline

Yard

Conductors in the yard, referred to as yard foremen, generally work on the ground under the supervision of a yardmaster. Yard foremen build and break trains and classify cars according to destination. In certain cases, the yardmaster provides overt instructions to the yard foreman regarding how to assemble the train. In other cases, the yardmaster will give the yard foreman a desired outcome (i.e., without explicitly stating the order of cars and the best way to switch them in and out) and the yard foreman must determine the most efficient way to make up the train while still adhering to car placement rules. Work in the yard is generally thought to be high risk, as compared with work on the mainline, because there is more time spent on the ground and around rolling equipment.

Local/Industry Jobs

Conductors working local/industry jobs are responsible for a mixture of yard work and over-the-road work. Local/industry jobs generally include operating between rail yards and industry sites, and picking up and setting out cars while servicing industries. Conductors spend time in the cab and on the ground. In the cab, conductors are responsible for similar tasks as long-haul mainline conductors, although local/industry jobs are shorter than long-haul operations, and therefore, the train crew may not encounter as many situations while en route. Conductors working industry jobs may also be required to switch cars while en route to ensure the train consist is in compliance with operating rules after setting out cars, so it is important that they acquire the skill set of yard foremen.

Long-Haul Mainline

Long-haul freight operations, as the name suggests, cover long distances and typically run from hub to hub, carrying freight over long distances with little or no pickups and set outs en route. Long-haul freight conductors require the skill set of yard foremen but also require skills for in-cab activities, which include the following: managing the train consist; coordinating with the locomotive engineer, interacting with dispatchers, roadway workers, and others outside the cab, dealing with exceptional situations (e.g., diagnosing and responding to train problems); and managing paperwork. Section 3.4 provides an overview of the overarching cognitive challenges associated with the work of conductors. Section 3.5 provides more in-depth discussion of the cognitive tasks and challenges associated with each of the five major categories of conductor work. For more information about freight conductor job tasks (i.e., the knowledge, skills, and abilities required to do the physical work), see Walsh et al. (2010).

3.4   Overarching Cognitive Challenges

Interviews with conductors and trainers revealed a number of environmental factors in which train crews operate that challenge cognitive and collaborative performance. These cognitive challenges place demands on conductor knowledge and long term memory, focus of attention, situation awareness, workload management, effective communication, and planning and decision making.

3.4.1 Large, Heterogeneous, and Dynamically Changing Territories

In order to work safely and efficiently, conductors as well as locomotive engineers are required to be familiar with the territory in which they operate. They need to remember, among other things, the location of grade crossings, control points, sidings, switches, and equipment defect detectors. Train crews must be familiar with the location of these objects in order to anticipate their approach well in advance. Train crews need to learn the norms of a territory to be able to make quick, calculated decisions about what action needs to be taken (e.g., knowing where a train of a certain length needs to stop to avoid blocking a grade crossing on a certain route).

One of the primary challenges relates to the size and complexity of the territory in which train crews are required to travel. Many conductors, particularly ones working long-haul mainline territories, may be required to operate over several subdivisions that may have varied topology, may include multiple industries, and go across multiple railroads with different methods of operation. Depending on their level of seniority and the size of the territory assigned, crews may be required to work in very different locations at different times; this makes learning the territory difficult.

An additional complication is that physical elements of the territory and rules applicable to the territory can change dynamically. For example, there may be temporary work zones or speed restrictions. There may also be permanent changes (e.g., relocation of signal appliances). Crews must remain vigilant to these changes. All these factors make it a challenge to anticipate and respond to what is ahead. Conductors repeatedly indicated that one of the ways they support locomotive engineers is by helping to fill in gaps in the locomotive engineer's knowledge of the territory. This is particularly the case when the locomotive engineer is new to the territory.

3.4.2 High Risk

Railroad workers must constantly maintain awareness of and guard against potential safety risks—to themselves and others.

Because part of conductors' responsibilities involves working on or around the track, they need to anticipate and avoid potential safety hazards. This includes learning how to safely work around equipment (e.g., the locomotive and cars). Conditions on the ground, including severe weather (e.g., extreme wind or snow), introduce additional risks to the conductor. This places a premium on the ability of conductors to maintain situation awareness of their environment as well as to learn and apply safe practices when standing and moving around equipment.

Working on or about moving equipment can be dangerous. Poor ergonomic design of train cars/equipment with awkwardly positioned hand and foot holds, pinch points, and opportunities to fall or be crushed contribute to safety hazards. This creates a need for conductors to learn "safe ways" to perform tasks and practice them until the behavior becomes automatic.

An added complication is that in some cases the safest way to perform a task may be less efficient, creating a temptation to take shortcuts that may be less safe. One of the points repeatedly made to us by managers and training instructors was the importance of convincing conductors that it is important to operate in a safe manner, even if it is perceived to be less efficient.

One of the hallmarks of more experienced conductors is that over time they learn efficient processes that are safe. For example, to avoid unnecessarily lifting and carrying a heavy knuckle over a long distance for installation in a particular car, conductors learn to drop the knuckle on the ground next to the locomotive and then have the train move forward until the car is aligned with where the knuckle was dropped. This avoids the risk of injury associated with carrying a heavy awkwardly shaped object.

Conductors also need to remain alert to safety risks of others and take action to mitigate them. This includes maintaining awareness of where grade crossings are (and the need to protect grade crossings as required) as well as awareness of potential risks to railroad workers along the right-of-way.

According to conductors, job safety briefings are one of the primary tools used to aid in anticipating and mitigating risk. Conductors and locomotive engineers perform these briefings at the start of every trip as well as immediately before each major activity of the day. Conductors also stressed the importance for job safety briefings to cover what each person is going to be doing, to review jointly potential safety hazards, and to develop plans to guard against these potential hazards.

3.4.3 Need for Sustained Vigilance

Another characteristic of train operations, which applies equally to conductors as well as locomotive engineers, is the need for sustained vigilance. The conductor needs to be continuously monitoring the track outside the cab to detect and call out signals, identify location of roadway workers, look for other trains or on-track vehicles, identify activities at grade crossings, as well as detect misaligned switches. In one dramatic example of the importance of vigilance outside the cab, a conductor saw that a car was going over a crossing as the train approached. It was close, but at first it did not alarm the crew, because they thought the car would be able to clear the crossing. Then, the conductor noticed that the reverse lights in the back of the car were illuminated. The train could not stop before hitting the car, but the conductor was able to alert the locomotive engineer in time to slow down and jump off the train.

Conductors are also responsible for monitoring parameters inside the locomotive cab such as train speed. If the locomotive engineer is speeding or fails to slow down in anticipation of a stop signal or end of authority, it is the responsibility of the conductor to warn the engineer of the need to slow down or stop, and if necessary to apply the emergency brake.

3.4.4 Workload Peaks and Demands for Multitasking

Train operations are characterized by workload transitions—long stretches of low workload punctuated by periods of high workload (Huey and Wickens, 1993; Wreathall et al., 2007). Particularly in the case of long-haul operations, there may be long stretches of track where there are no events that require explicit action by the conductor. However, conductors stressed that workload peak situations regularly arise that require multitasking on their part. These situations generally involve the need to monitor outside the cab while communicating with others (e.g., a dispatcher) and simultaneously recording information (e.g., filling out a signal awareness form, copying a track warrant, or updating a train list).

For example, conductors routinely need to communicate via radio with others who are remotely located (e.g., a dispatcher or roadway supervisor) to obtain and document movement instructions (e.g., to obtain track warrants, slow orders, authority to enter a work zone, or changes in work plans). In those cases, the conductor needs to monitor events outside the cab, talking over the radio, documenting information, and passing it on to the locomotive engineer, all at the same time. The need for this multitasking was described eloquently by one conductor:

> "The dispatcher gives you track warrant authority. While he is giving you this information you have to record it and then read it back to him over the radio when he is done. He has to acknowledge if it is correct or if you need to repeat it again. After you get the track warrant you have to read it to the locomotive engineer and brief with him where your limits are on that track warrant and any restrictions that

the dispatcher listed on that track warrant. Also you are still writing signals down. And the train is still moving. You need to still be looking and listening."

Conductors repeatedly pointed out that these situations pose challenges for less experienced conductors. The ability to effectively multitask in these types of situations develops with experience.

3.4.5 Rare Events

Conductors are responsible for handling nonroutine events. In particular, they are responsible for troubleshooting train equipment malfunctions and fixing them. Any specific malfunction is likely to happen with low frequency. For example, conductors are taught how to change a broken knuckle as part of initial classroom training. However, broken knuckles happen very rarely on the road. One conductor mentioned that in his 7-year career, he never had to change a knuckle. Because the events happen with low frequency, it may have been years since they received training on how to handle the event. Furthermore, because the possible range of events that may arise with low frequency, conductors are unlikely to have been exposed to them as part of their OJT. This means that when these events occur, the conductors may be facing the situation for the first time.

3.4.6 Actual (or Perceived) Time Pressure

One of the primary responsibilities of a train crew is to keep the train moving. Although railroads may have explicit policies in place stressing that safety always comes first, situations can arise where train crews feel compromised by competing imperatives. For example they may feel pressured to reach a location or complete a task before hours of service limits are reached. Conductors repeatedly mentioned that perception of time pressure can cause some individuals to rush or take short cuts that can reduce safety margins.

3.4.7 Information Overload

Conductors repeatedly mentioned the need to keep up with a lot of rapidly changing information. This includes daily bulletins that provide dynamic updates such as locations of work zones or temporary speed restrictions, published timetables that provide information on train schedules, and rule books that document the operating rules for particular railroads over whose territories they cross.

Conductors mentioned that one of the challenges they confront is the need to keep up with rule changes. Depending on the territory, conductors may need to maintain awareness of and comply with rules from multiple rule books. This occurs when routes go across territory of other railroads (i.e., foreign territory) that use different rule books.

Conductors are required to review rule changes prior to a trip. Although this is important for ensuring that they are aware of the rule change, it does not guarantee that they will remember it or recognize that it applies when confronted with the applicable situation (this is particularly the case if the situation occurs rarely).

Conductors have developed a variety of "homegrown" strategies for keeping up with dynamically changing information. These are described in Section 3.6.7.

3.4.8 Fatigue

Conductors repeatedly mentioned working when fatigued as a major challenge. A major contributor to fatigue is the unpredictable work schedules that are required in the industry to sustain 24/7 operations. Conductors, particularly those with lower seniority as a result of shorter job tenure, are often called into service with very short notice, making it more difficult to ensure they are rested prior to starting their shift. Hours of service (HOS) rules from the RSIA specify that a railroad employee may only be on-duty if that employee has had at least 10 consecutive hours off during the last 24 hours and cannot go on-duty if that employee has been on-duty for 6 consecutive days. However, because HOS regulations do not consider employees' commute times to and from their job and cannot regulate what a conductor does during time off, a common struggle among those with unpredictable work hours is balancing their need for sleep (both in terms of quality and quantity) with other personal obligations such as social and/or family concerns.

Lack of rest prior to a shift coupled with the train movement can lead to loss of alertness and vulnerability to falling asleep, particularly on long stretches with little explicit activity required. Conductors and locomotive engineers made a point of stressing the important role that crewmembers played in keeping each other alert in those situations. Frings (2011) reinforces this concept in his research by noting that working as part of a team can help offset the effects of fatigue on performance.

3.5 Cognitive Tasks and Associated Challenges

In this section, we examine the major cognitive tasks and challenges associated with the conductor's work in more depth. This CTA focuses on the cognitive aspects of the conductor's job, which we divide into five primary categories:

- Managing the train consist
- Coordinating with the locomotive engineer for safe and efficient en route operation
- Dealing with exceptional situations (e.g., diagnosing and responding to train problems)
- Interacting with dispatchers/roadway workers and others outside the cab
- Managing paperwork

3.5.1 Managing the Train Consist

Conductors on the mainline are responsible for managing the train consist, which includes ensuring that the order of cars is in compliance with placement rules. This requires consideration of car content (e.g., hazardous materials), weight (e.g., loaded cars versus empties), and dimension (e.g., wide loads and high cars).

Conductors need to understand the impact of cargo type on car placement to ensure that the train is made up correctly. Prior to departing the yard, conductors look over the train car placement list to ensure that the train is in compliance with all car placement rules. Conductors agreed that it is rare to come upon a train that was made up incorrectly in the yard, because those errors are usually caught by the computer; however, it does happen.

When evaluating car placement, conductors also need to consider the sequence in which cars will be set out en route. Cars to be set out at different locations need to be grouped properly based on set out location in addition to car consist, weight, and dimension. Experienced conductors learn to place cars next to each other for easy set outs at industry sidings; also, conductors are able to think ahead to ensure that after those cars are set out the remaining cars are still in compliance with car placement rules.

Once on the road, conductors need to ensure that the train consist remains in compliance with car placement rules as cars are set out or picked up. For example, if after setting out cars at industry, a car containing hazmat is within five cars of the locomotive, or is placed next to a load that may shift, the consist is no longer in compliance with operating rules, and the conductor must rearrange the cars before the train can proceed.

Conductors need to be cognizant of car placement even on runs that do not include preplanned en route set outs and pickups. For example, if an unanticipated event, such as the activation of a hot box detector, occurs and results in removing or rearranging equipment, the conductor must be cognizant of the implications of setting out that car:

- Will setting out that car put a car with hazmat too close to the engine?
- Will it disrupt the order of cars such that a helper locomotive is now too close to the front of the train?
- How will it affect the train's weight and length, and what are the implications of this on how the engineer must operate the train?

Understanding how to properly manage train consist ensures that when these unanticipated situations arise the conductor can take action and fix the problem.

Conductors on the mainline must also understand the impact of train consist and makeup on train operations. A train's consist may dictate its allowable speed or route. Train length and weight impact allowable train speed, and certain car sizes (i.e., wide or high loads) may affect clearance of the train with respect to bridges or equipment operating on adjacent tracks. For example, a "key" train (a train carrying a specified number of loaded rail cars, trailers, or containers of hazmat) has several operating restrictions, including restrictions on maximum allowable speed, specific rules regarding communication with the dispatcher, and restrictions on entering certain sidings. Conductors must be cognizant of these things to ensure locomotive engineer compliance when operating the train.

3.5.2 Coordinating with the Locomotive Engineer for Safe and Efficient En Route Operation

Once en route, one of the conductor's main task is to supervise the operation and administration of the train to ensure safe and efficient operation and compliance with all operating rules. Achieving this objective requires close coordination with the locomotive engineer. Conductors handle all radio communication and take care of paperwork when the train is in motion so that the locomotive engineer can concentrate on operating the train. In addition, the conductor provides essential support and backup for the locomotive engineer.

The conductor reminds the engineer about upcoming signals and slow orders and provides look ahead information to alert the engineer to hills, curves, grade crossings, etc. The conductor also actively monitors outside the cab, calling out signals and alerting locomotive engineers to potential hazards. This is important because, in addition to serving as a backup/reminder to the locomotive engineer, conductors noted that in some cases they may have a slightly different line of sight and therefore may be able to detect signals, trespassers, or hazards on the track that are visible from their side of the locomotive cab slightly before they become visible from the engineer's side.

The conductor is also responsible for monitoring the performance of the locomotive engineer to ensure safety and compliance with all operating rules. In particular, if the conductor feels that the train is not being operated safely, the conductor must alert the engineer or apply the emergency brake if necessary. While the locomotive engineer has full control over operating the train, the conductor is responsible for pulling the emergency brake to bring the train to a stop if the conductor feels personal safety, the train, or others outside the train are in danger.

3.5.3 Dealing with Exceptional Situations

Learning to handle an unexpected situation is part of working effectively on the mainline. Unexpected situations include anything from train equipment malfunctions to unanticipated work en route to collisions and derailments. Although they run the gamut, train equipment issues are perhaps the most common unanticipated events that arise en route, and in these cases, it is the conductor who is responsible for troubleshooting and, if possible, repairing the train.

When discussing their role on the mainline, all conductors interviewed brought up the need to troubleshoot and repair equipment. Conductors discussed the potential for broken knuckles, broken drawbars, broken rear end devices, and bad orders, among others.

3.5.4 Interacting with Dispatchers and Others outside the Cab

Train crews rely on frequent communication with dispatchers, other trains, and roadway workers to ensure safe operation of the train. It is the conductor's job to manage these radio communications, which often includes copying down train orders communicated over the radio and repeating them back to the dispatcher.

3.5.5 Managing Paperwork

Conductors are required to fill out and maintain all paperwork for the train, including track warrants, work orders, train consist, etc. At the start of a shift, the conductor's duty is to gather all the paperwork and make two copies, one for him/herself and one for the engineer, look it over, and check for errors. Paperwork contains information about the train's consist, equipment, and trip information that conductors must review to identify special requirements for the trip. Conductors agreed that car placement errors are rare because a computer generally catches them, but there are other errors that experience has taught them to identify. For example, one conductor mentioned the need to look at the weight of the train to determine the maximum allowable speed rather than relying on the paperwork alone. Often, with loaded grain trains, the weight of the train is too heavy to run the train at the typical maximum allowable speed, but the paperwork does not take the train weight into consideration, only train type. That same conductor also mentioned the need to check axle counts against the paperwork. If they do not match up, it could mean that a car is missing or that, unbeknownst to the train crew, an extra car was attached to the train.

In addition to maintaining paperwork relating to the trip, the conductor must stay current on the railroad's rulebook. Rulebooks can change on a weekly, sometimes daily, basis. To avoid rule violations, conductors check for rule updates prior to boarding the train and then integrate the new rule into their books. Rule changes are issued in email bulletins and/or uploaded electronically on the railroad's Web site. Some conductors opt to print rule changes out and add them to their rulebook; others bring electronic versions (on PDAs or laptops).

While en route, the conductor is responsible for documenting the trip in a log. This includes writing down slow orders and authorizations from the dispatcher and recording signals as they are passed, as well as filling out other forms as necessary (e.g., updating train list when picking up or setting our cars, filling out form Bs when dealing with maintenance-of-way, etc.). This activity must be done while also communicating with the engineer and dispatcher, as necessary, and looking out the window for signals, curves, trespassers, etc.

3.5.6 Additional Cognitive Demands in Mountain Grade Territory

Interviews with conductors revealed that not all mainline freight operations are the same. Working in mountain grade territory in particular has the potential to increase the complexity of the job of conductors as well as locomotive engineers because of the additional variables that need to be accounted for when operating the train (described below). On mountain grade territory, as opposed to flat terrain, conductors have additional car placement and train handling concerns that contribute to complexity. One conductor working on tracks that run through the Blue Mountains in Oregon spoke at length about the importance of train makeup when operating on mountain grade territory. Train length and tonnage determine allowable car type and placement on trains operating over heavy grades. For example, on a heavy train a car weighing less than 45 tons cannot be within the first 15 cars of the train, regardless of cargo type. Paying extra attention to placement of loads and empties is also important, as well as placement of hazmat. Train makeup is further complicated because trains operating on mountain grade may require one or more distributed power units (DPU). DPUs have additional placement rules and restrictions, which are dependent on the locomotive tonnage and mountain grade operated on.

That same conductor also mentioned the importance of tying hand brakes on trains operating over mountain grade. Tying hand brakes is crucial to ensure the train does not roll away while stopped on a grade, and more hand brakes are needed when the train is on a steep grade than when the train is on flat territory. The number of hand brakes necessary is determined by a matrix of factors that depends on the train's tonnage and the grade over which the train is operating. Conductors interviewed noted that tying hand brakes is more of a physical demand than a cognitive demand. The need for additional hand brakes adds additional complexity to situations where equipment breaks, because tying more hand brakes are necessary. For example, in the case of a broken knuckle when the train is in mountain grade territory and going downhill, the conductor must tie the train down with enough hand brakes to ensure that when the engineer cuts the air in, the airbrakes are not going to release.

Another example of additional complexities in mountain grade territory is loss of communication with the end-of-train (EOT) device. In flat territory, if the head end loses communication with the EOT, the train can continue on at a reduced speed of 30 mph. When the head end loses communication with the EOT in mountain grade territory, the train can only go one train length. If after one train length communication with the EOT is not recovered, the engineer is required to stop the train, and the conductor must walk from the head end to the EOT at the rear end of the train and troubleshoot the problem. At that point the conductor, alone in the EOT, is responsible for deciding what course of action to take: stop the train and wait for help, or cut the train in half, take half the train up the hill, and then come back and put the locomotive on the rear of the train and continue.

Finally, in mountain grade territory, a factor that contributes to the complexity of the job is that there is less margin for error. Conductors know they have to be more vigilant and remain alert when operating on a mountain grade because the possibility for an unanticipated event happening on that part of the route is greater than on flat terrain because of additional forces acting on the train. Therefore, the need for sustained attention is important because incidents can escalate quickly with less time for correction. On mountain grade territory, as opposed to flat territory, trains going uphill are at risk of stalling on the track. Conversely, heavy trains going downhill are susceptible to overspeed and derailment. For example, a heavy train going downhill is liable to pick up speed extremely quickly if the train crew is not vigilant, which introduces the possibility of a derailment. For this reason in mountain grade territory, if the train is 5 mph over the speed limit, the train must be put into emergency. If a conductor sees that the train is going toward overspeed (e.g., the train is going 44 mph in a 45-mile per hour zone while going downhill) and the engineer has not taken action to slow the train, the conductor can apply the emergency brake. As one conductor stated, an extra 30 seconds can make all the difference between safely stopping the train and a derailment. Having less margin for error and therefore a need to think and act swiftly, combined with a complex task like operating the train in mountain grade territory, can create dangerous situations.

3.6   Overarching Knowledge and Cognitive Skill Requirements for Expert Performances

Although experience is gained on a continuum, interviews with conductors and trainers indicate that it can take up to 5 years to gain sufficient experience to become an expert conductor. Experienced conductors, as is the case in most professions, have a greater store of knowledge because of their time spent working in the industry and are able to respond more quickly to situations than less experienced conductors. In this section we summarize the types of knowledge and cognitive skills that conductors develop, largely through on-the-job experience, that enable them to operate more safely and efficiently. This knowledge and skills differentiate expert conductors from inexperienced conductors. They represent the types of knowledge and skills that may be useful to focus on during initial and OJT so as to more rapidly develop expertise.

Conductors build certain skills through repeated practice and experience with a particular task until it becomes more automatic, requiring less sustained attention to perform (Schneider and

Shiffrin, 1977). One example of the kind of skill acquired over time is the ability to multitask in high workload situations, such as when conductors need to listen to the radio while simultaneously monitoring out the window and writing down information being communicated. Another example is the ability to listen for and accurately interpret radio communication. Dispatchers often speak quickly, and conductors require repeated practice to understand and efficiently write down information communicated over a noisy radio channel.

Other aspects of expertise depend on knowledge that is developed through first-hand experience with a range of specific situations. For example, the first time a conductor enters a specific location with a complex configuration of multiple switches, he may have difficulty determining the appropriate switch to line up . Once the conductor becomes familiar with that particular location, he or she will know which switch to line up with right away and therefore will get the job done more efficiently.

Conductors stressed that first-hand experience in the field was important for converting "book knowledge" that was learned in the classroom to integrated skills that could be confidently applied. For example, one conductor mentioned that individuals may have learned how to cut a car out as part of their initial training, but if they have never done it themselves, they may not be able to do so the first time.

The importance of first-hand experience was particularly stressed when identifying potential hazards in the environment and developing strategies for operating safely. Several conductors mentioned that experiencing "close calls" enabled conductors to appreciate the potential for danger and to develop strategies to avoid or mitigate risk when faced with similar situations (e.g., knowing how many hand brakes to tie). Less experienced conductors may underestimate how many hand brakes they need to tie or may release them prematurely. More experienced conductors are more likely to appreciate the potential risk and take added precautions to reduce risk. For example, they may not only test the hand brakes but also block the wheels just in case the hand brakes do not work.

First-hand experience with rarely occurring situations was identified as one of the benefits of having a conductor and a locomotive engineer on a train. The availability of two individuals broadened the set of experiences that could be drawn upon when confronting a relatively rare situation. A relatively inexperienced conductor could benefit from the knowledge of a more experienced locomotive engineer and vice versa.

3.6.1 Knowledge of the Territory

Knowledge of the territory provides the foundation for being able to operate safely and efficiently. It is the locomotive engineer's primary responsibility to operate the train; therefore, he or she must be intimately familiar with the territory. It is also important for conductors to have sufficient knowledge of the territory to enable them to ensure train compliance at all times. Train crews need to develop a detailed mental model of the physical territory in which they operate. This includes knowledge of territory grade, location of signals, milepost signs, grade crossings, landmarks, sidings, switches and detectors, as well as knowledge of track layout of yards and location of industries. This detailed knowledge takes time to acquire.

Knowledge of the territory also includes learning conventions related to how to approach a location (e.g., a siding, an industry), where to start braking (e.g., if coming to a tight turn or steep grade), and where to stop for safe and efficient performance. An example often provided is where to stop so as not to block a crossing.

Another example is whether to approach an industry siding with the cars to be dropped off in front or behind the engine. A conductor mentioned a case in which he had to go to an industry location that was 3 miles away because he was unfamiliar with how to set out cars. He and the engineer proceeded to pull the cars behind the engine to the industry location only to discover that there was no turnaround once they entered the industry track. Instead of dragging the cars behind the engine, they should have shoved the cars (backing in) so that they would be able to drop off the cars and pull back out of the industry track.

As will be illustrated by examples in the following sections, knowledge of the territory is critical to enabling train crews to operate efficiently as well as to anticipate and mitigate risks to themselves and others.

3.6.2 Ability to Maintain Situation Awareness of Surroundings

A cognitive skill that depends critically on knowledge of the territory is the ability to develop and maintain situation awareness of one's surroundings. Conductors repeatedly indicated that awareness of your surroundings and the ability to anticipate and avoid potential hazards is one of the skills that distinguish more experienced conductors from less experienced conductors.

Conductors need to continuously monitor their surroundings whether they are in the locomotive or switching cars on the ground. They need to maintain awareness of the location of other trains and machines on the track, the location of cars and whether these cars are secured, and the location of people working on or around the track.

As in the case of engineers, conductors need to monitor the composition of their train consist relative to key elements in the environment. For example, they need to maintain awareness of the location of the front and back of the train relative to grade crossings or speed restriction zones. Conductors need to know whether their train will fit without blocking a crossing. If their consist includes high cars, they need to be aware of the location of close clearances such as bridges and pillars. If their consist includes wide loads, they need to maintain awareness of narrow clearances as well as the location of meets with other trains (that may also have wide loads).

Knowledge of the surroundings is particularly important when working on the ground around a train or walking to or from the train. Conductors stressed that when coupling cars or otherwise working around the train, it is critical to be aware of where you are standing or moving relative to the "red zone." The red zone is defined as an arm's distance from the track. If you are within the red zone you can be struck by a car or engine. The red zone exists regardless of whether there is equipment on the track. If a conductor needs to step into the red zone, for example, to couple two cars together, the conductor must first ensure that the engineer sets the brakes and centers the reverser handle to ensure that the train will not move. This is referred to as "set and center." Conductors indicated that losing awareness of where they are relative to the red zone is one of the major causes of accidents.

Walking on the ground to get to and from rail cars also poses hazards. Such situations arise, for example, if a detector indicates a fault, and the conductor needs to walk the train to identify the cause of the problem. When walking on the ground, it is important to be aware of the walking conditions and to anticipate and avoid potential hazards. For example, conductors mentioned tall grass that can obstruct a person's view, inclined grading that can make it easier to lose footing, tripping hazards, and threatening animals.

3.6.3 Ability to Project Effect of Consist on Train Dynamics

One of the skills conductors develop with experience is the ability to estimate the impact of consist characteristics (e.g., number of cars, length, weight) on train dynamics. Consist characteristics impact train handling. For example, the number of cars and whether they are empty or full influences how quickly a train can speed up or slow down, particularly in territory with steep grades. Although the locomotive engineer is directly responsible for operating the train, the conductor is responsible for overseeing safe operation of the train. Therefore, conductors as well as locomotive engineers must understand the impact of train consist and need to be able to project the impact of the train consist on train dynamics. This skill is particularly required in situations where the train is making a backup move with the conductor positioned in the back of the train providing direction to the locomotive engineer who is up front and cannot see the back of the train. In those situations, the conductor needs to be able to estimate how many car lengths are required to stop the train so that he can effectively guide the locomotive engineer.

Experienced conductors are better than less experienced conductors at estimating the impact of train consist on the distance required to stop the train.

3.6.4 Ability to Problem Solve

It is important for a conductor to be a "problem-solver." Conductors routinely confront novel situations where they perform mental simulations to identify a correct solution. This skill develops with experience.

As one conductor noted: "A good conductor to me is a problem solver…When I first hired out…I had to learn how to figure out 12 hours of work in my head and knowing multiple moves to keep the job moving. Not everyone can do that." He used playing chess as an analogy to explain that the problem solving required involves mental simulation and "look ahead" and requires time and experience to develop: "It comes back to chess. A new guy won't be as good as the experienced guy. Can't teach you to be a good chess player. It takes time and experience."

The clearest example of problem solving performed by conductors that requires mental simulation is the reasoning required to determine the most appropriate sequence of train cars. Determining the placement order of cars in a train is referred to as building the train consist. Although, at large yards, it is the yardmaster who plans out the placement order of cars on a train, there remain situations where it is the conductor who needs to develop and/or evaluate the placement of cars in a train consist. For example, in smaller yards without yardmasters, the conductor is responsible for planning out and building the train consist. Similarly, situations often arise once en route where cars need to be set out or added to the train consist. In those situations, the conductor must evaluate car placement and, if necessary, switch cars around to build an appropriate consist.

When building the train consist, conductors need to make sure that the sequence of cars (1) does not violate any rules and (2) will enable cars to be set out and picked up en route with minimal need to switch cars around once on the mainline.

Conductors need to consider several rules when deciding upon, or evaluating, the order of cars in a train. One of the most important rules relates to the placement of cars that contain hazardous materials (referred to as hazmat). For example, there generally needs to be five nonhazardous cars between a locomotive and a hazmat car. There are also rules about relative position of cars of different lengths and different weights as well as the relative position of shiftable loads.

Conductors stated there are now computer programs that can review a train consist list and flag rule violations (e.g., a hazmat car that is too close to a locomotive engine). However, these computer programs are used to check the train consist once it is built. The conductor still needs to build the train consist, which requires mental manipulation of car positions to come up with a train makeup that is in compliance with all car placement rules. As one conductor explained: "The computer will tell you if you did it wrong (e.g., short car next to a long car) but an experienced person can figure it out without looking at their paper work while you are switching…short car shouldn't be next to an 85 foot car, it should be between these other cars that are 50 foot."

The need for problem-solving particularly arises when setting out and picking up cars on the mainline. When picking up cars, the conductor needs to consider whether they contain hazardous materials, as well as their length and weight (e.g., are they loads or empties) in determining where to place the cars in the train. Similarly, when setting out cars, the conductor needs to be able to reevaluate the makeup of the remaining cars. Experienced conductors will evaluate the impact of changes to the consist and decide whether cars need to be switched around. Less experienced conductors may not recognize problems with the consist. As one conductor explained,

> "From experience if I'm going on duty and my cars list 1–100, and I know I have five cars to set out, automatically in my head I'm looking at the next five to see what I have to do after I set them out. I know that because I've been out here for a while, but a new guy may not know to look at the next five to make sure when he sets out (some cars) they are going to be good or not."

Conductors are faced with other types of problem situations as well. Most notably they are responsible for handling emergency situations that may arise on the road. If an emergency occurs, they have to troubleshoot the source of the problem, which requires them to walk the train and know what to look for, how to look for it, and what to do in response. An example of a malfunction is a sticky airbrake valve. As a result, when the locomotive engineer sets the brakes the air pressure completely exhausts, effectively stopping the train instead of shoving it. The conductor has to identify which car has the problem and cut the brakes out on that car. Another possibility is the uncoupling of an air hose. In that case, the conductor has to locate the problem and reconnect the air hose.

Other common situations are when a hot-box detector identifies a defect. The conductor needs to identify the car with the problem and determine whether it needs to be set out. If so, then the conductor needs to determine an appropriate location to set the car out, how fast the train can go until reaching that location, and how to secure the rest of the train when setting out the car. The conductor must also determine the impact of removing that car on the remaining train consist. Removing that car may cause the remaining train consist to be improperly sequenced (e.g., if you removed a car that resulted in a hazmat car being less than five cars away from a locomotive engine). A less experienced conductor may set the car out and keep going without realizing that removing the car created a problem, whereas an experienced conductor would recognize the need to switch cars around.

3.6.5 Ability to Plan Ahead

Conductors indicated that one of the primary cognitive challenges of working on the mainline is the need to constantly think ahead. Conductors need to anticipate and prepare for what is coming next on the road (e.g., signals, curves, grade crossings, train meets). It is also important to think ahead about various tasks they will need to accomplish over the shift so as to plan the most safe and efficient way to accomplish them.

Because conductors and locomotive engineers work together, some of the examples provided by the conductors are situations that locomotive engineers are responsible for as well. For example, conductors and locomotive engineers need to anticipate likely upcoming signals and think through implications for when and where to stop the train. One conductor provided a specific example that illustrates this point. He described a track location where there was a signal that was followed by two grade crossings and then another signal that occurred immediately after a curve in the track. The first signal was yellow. In his words,

> "You are almost sure you will get a red signal next, but can't see it. It is around a curve. Where do I stop?....We are probably going to meet a train. That is why we are stopping. Will my train fit between the road crossings without blocking? Where I stop depends on how long the train is...will we fit between the road crossings, if not, then maybe we should stop at the yellow signal. This is the communication that needs to take place [between the conductor and the locomotive engineer]."

This example makes clear that conductors and engineers need to anticipate and plan ahead. In this case, they needed to anticipate the upcoming signal and decide where to stop based on consideration of characteristics of the upcoming territory (Are there curves? When will the next signal be visible? Are there places on the upcoming track where it would be inappropriate to stop?) as well as characteristics of their train (e.g., How long is the train? Can it fit between the two grade crossings or will it block one?) and the likely reason for and length of the stop.

A second example illustrates how thinking ahead allows experienced conductors to increase work efficiency as well as safety. A conductor needed to set out some cars. The question the conductor confronted was where to stop the train given that the train was on the side of a hill. In his words,

"Say we're on a hill. Where do we tie the train down?....Maybe put it in a place where you don't have to secure it as much as you would on the side of a hill. That is experience. If I'm on the main track and I have to make a set out, I might set it out a mile away where it is flat, and I'll only have to tie five hand breaks to hold it, versus pulling up on the side of the hill where I have to tie 25 hand brakes to hold it."

This case illustrates that experienced conductors think through the implications of stopping at different locations (on a hill versus flat track) and plan ahead where to stop to maximize safety and efficiency. The issue involved in this case was the number of hand brakes that would need to be tied to safely secure the train on a hill versus a flat location. Thinking ahead enabled the conductor to recognize that he could stop at a flat location that required fewer hand brakes to be tied to safely secure the train, thus increasing both safety and efficiency.

Another type of situation where thinking ahead is required is planning how best to approach an industry siding to set out cars. As was described earlier, different industry locations may have different track profiles. In some cases, the track layout at the industry location does not allow the train to turnaround. In those cases, to set out cars, the crew needs to shove the cars (with the train pushing) rather than pulling the cars. Experienced conductors will most likely be familiar with the industry locations in their territory and will anticipate whether the cars will need to be shoved or pulled. If an experienced conductor is assigned a job to set out cars at an unfamiliar location, the conductor will consult a track profile of the industry siding, which is a schematic diagram that maps the track layout for that industry location. The conductor will review the track profile prior to starting the trip to plan how the train will need to approach the industry.

Another instance where experienced conductors think ahead relates to thinking through the most efficient sequence of cars when building a train consist. An experienced conductor will plan what cars will be dropped off and picked up and in what order when initially deciding how to build the train. This kind of planning minimizes the need for reordering cars en route. One example is to group the cars in order of the location they will be dropped off so as to minimize the need to switch cars in and out once on the road. Thinking ahead improves efficiency by minimizing the need to switch cars in route.

3.6.6 Ability to Multitask

Another skill that differentiates more experienced from less experienced conductors is the ability to effectively manage multiple demands on attention. Several conductors mentioned that situations routinely arise where they need to be simultaneously listening to radio communication, documenting authorities provided, communicating those authorities to the locomotive engineer, and monitoring the environment outside the window, all while the train is moving.

One conductor gave a good example of the need to multitask:

"Dispatcher calls you as you're coming up to a siding. You have signals, clear advance approach, approach, and then a red. Say you pass an advance approach. Need to call out "cab red zone." All of a sudden dispatcher calls you, and says I've got something for you. You're trying to make sure the engineer is slowing down, copying down what the dispatcher is telling you, and talking on the radio, and all this time you've been running 60 mph, you have 6 miles to stop, and you just passed an advance approach and approach is coming up so you're getting up on 4 miles, and you need to copy back to the dispatcher and give the information to the engineer. Horns are blowing, making it hard to hear, and you're filling out the conductor log. There's a lot that goes on. It's a matter of taking a deep breath and doing it."

Experienced conductors have learned strategies for managing and prioritizing these competing demands on their attention.

3.6.7 Ability to Exploit External Memory Aids

As was mentioned in Section 3.4, mainline operations place heavy demands on memory. This includes the need to remember operating rules and particularly changes to operating rules; the need to be familiar with the territory; and the need to remember changes such as temporary speed restrictions and work zones that are published in daily bulletins.

Conductors have developed several strategies for keeping up with rule book changes. One approach is to download electronic versions of the rule book that incorporate the latest changes. These can be downloaded onto a portable computer or PDA that can be brought onboard the train. Some conductors download an electronic version of the entire rule book. Others download a list of the rules that have recently changed. Other conductors print out new and revised rules and use these to update personal notebooks of rule changes.

Conductors have also developed strategies to support *prospective memory*. Prospective memory is memory for things that need to be accomplished in the future. An example of prospective memory is remembering upcoming temporary speed restrictions or work zones. Temporary speed restrictions and work zones are communicated in bulletins that the conductors are required to print out at the start of their shifts. However, the bulletins may list many temporary changes, not all of which will apply to their specific route. Experienced conductors have developed a number of strategies to focus their attention on the specific temporary speed restrictions and work zones that are relevant to their particular trip. Some conductors underline or highlight the relevant temporary speed restrictions and work zones. Others write them down on a separate sheet. Conductors may also cross out items as locations are passed, further focusing their attention on the upcoming ones. These various techniques all represent strategies that rely on external aids to support prospective memory.

Experienced conductors also rely on maps as a way to supplement their knowledge of the territory. This includes maps and fog charts that provide schematic representations of the track that show important territory features such as grades, curves, and crossings. There are also job profiles that provide detailed graphic representation of how the track is laid out at specific industry locations. Many maps are available for download from railroad Web sites. Experienced conductors will print out relevant maps prior to the start of a trip, particularly if they are less familiar with that particular location. They will review the maps with the locomotive engineer as necessary as part of the initial job brief.

Ability to Foster Shared Situation Awareness through Active Communication

Conductors need to communicate effectively with the locomotive engineer as well as other members of the train crew to maintain shared situation awareness, facilitate efficient work, and enhance safety. They also need to communicate effectively with others via radio, including dispatchers and roadway workers. Conductors indicated that effective communication is learned through experience.

Communication with the locomotive engineer is important to maintain shared situation awareness of the current environment, activities, plans, and intentions. Conductors indicated that communication with the locomotive engineer needs to be an active ongoing process. It begins with the initial job brief when they come on duty but also includes ongoing communication as they are traveling on the mainline and intermediate job briefs that are informally initiated prior to performing particularly challenging tasks. This concept was referred to as a "rolling" job brief.

An initial job brief occurs when the conductor and engineer first come on duty. They review all the paperwork and discuss the tasks ahead and how they plan to accomplish them. The goal is to make sure that they have a shared understanding of the work, the rules that apply, and the potential risks to be aware of. It is during this initial job brief that they will discuss their level of experience and how familiar each is with the territory. They may also pull up and review maps and industry job profiles, if they are less familiar with the territory, as well as obtain advice from others who may be more familiar with the territory. They will also discuss any rule changes to make sure they both know them and how they may apply to the upcoming trip. This initial job brief enables the crew to gain a shared understanding of one another's knowledge and abilities as well as shared expectations of the work ahead.

Once on the mainline, the conductor will engage in active communication to support the engineer in maintaining situation awareness of where they are, and what is coming up next, and awareness of signals, speed restrictions, and work zones. Conductors are required by rule to call out signals and confirm that the locomotive engineer has acknowledged them. Experienced conductors will also make sure that the locomotive engineer is aware of key upcoming features of the territory (e.g., curves, hills, grade crossings), particularly if the territory is unfamiliar. As one conductor explained, "When you come on duty you should get as familiar with your coworker for that day as you can. Understand what he knows about that territory. If he has been on it once, twice, how many times has he had a pilot, how comfortable is he?" An experienced conductor, riding with an engineer who is less familiar with the territory, will engage in communication to ensure that the engineer is aware of where they are and what to anticipate next. If necessary the conductor will pull out track maps and keep the engineer informed of critical upcoming features such as curves, hills, and grade crossings that may require them to begin reducing speed ahead of time.

In their general role of overseeing safe train operations, experienced conductors will also communicate and participate in decisionmaking with respect to when to begin slowing down or where best to stop the train (e.g., when approaching a red signal). This is particularly true when the engineer is less familiar with the territory. Although it is the locomotive engineer's primary job to operate the train and know when and where to begin slowing the train down, the conductor and engineer work together as a team, sharing knowledge and experience to ensure optimal train operation. As one conductor stated,

> "If I have this new engineer...it's almost like I'm doing both jobs. I need to make sure he knows where everything is. He really don't know, say if you are going to meet a train somewhere. If your train is a certain length, can your train fit without blocking a crossing? What is the norm for the territory to keep you from getting in trouble? Because the engineer doesn't know the territory. Sometimes there are certain places that are the norm for a territory, if you're a certain length you don't want to block a crossing for hours, need to know where you are, and where you can stop."

Experienced conductors will also ensure that the locomotive engineer is aware of all radio communication with dispatchers and roadway workers and that the locomotive engineer has actively been consulted prior to responding to any requests made over the radio (e.g., requests to take back track authorities). Less experienced conductors may not always appreciate the need to explicitly consult with the engineer prior to responding to a radio request. As one conductor explained,

> "A lot of times with a new conductor, especially a guy right out of class, when the dispatcher calls they get so nervous, really tense. One issue was a dispatcher calling and asking, can I have a signal back at such and such location. Under that nervous pressure, conductor will sometime mess up because they want to answer fast, not realizing the importance of understanding what the dispatcher is asking for. Communication between the two crew members on that cab should be at the top of the agenda at that point. When the dispatcher calls and asks can I have the signal back at such and such, that means the dispatcher is going to put a red block. Possibly change your route or hold you there for just a bit. If you're not exactly proof positive of where that location is, do not give that signal to the dispatcher. Need to hold off on that until you're sure you know where you are. You need to have a job briefing. Need to ask engineer, can you stop this train at this location before I give this signal back to the dispatcher. When dispatcher is asking can I have that signal back, he's asking the crew....When the engineer is running the train, he can't be on the radio. The engineer can hear the dispatcher on the radio. Everybody hears. But it doesn't hurt to say hey, did you hear that. Every time the dispatcher asks, I look at engineer, and he nods his head. That's an acknowledgement that he heard and we're on the same page."

Effective communication between the crew regarding train movement is paramount. This includes situations where cars are being set out, picked up, or switched, where cars are being shoved, and situations where cars on the train need to be secured. In those cases, the conductor may be on the ground or in the back of the train and communicating with the engineer over radio or with hand signals. In those situations, close, unambiguous communication between the locomotive engineer and conductor is critical so that they are jointly aware of where each one is and what each is going to do. One example is when cars are being shoved into place requiring the train to back up. In those cases, the locomotive engineer may not be able to see the end of the train or know where the conductor is positioned. This can be a dangerous situation. As one conductor eloquently explained, in those types of scenarios, it is important for the conductor to "paint a picture for the engineer." It is important to let the engineer know where the conductor is, where the train needs to stop (e.g., we are 10 cars away from our stop), and what obstacles might be in the path (e.g., there is a derail in two cars so we need to stop short).

Conductors indicated that it is particularly important to engage in discussions of potential risks and hazards associated with an upcoming job. These risks may include walking conditions, elements that may obstruct vision such as tall grass, slippery handholds or footholds, people and equipment on the track, and unsecured cars. This is an area that they felt was insufficiently covered during current training and that less experienced conductors may not know to discuss in a job briefing. Currently, the focus of job briefings is on the technical work to be performed. Conductors felt it was equally important to be able to identify and discuss potential risks and how they plan to mitigate those risks. As one conductor indicated,

> "Currently a normal job briefing is just talking about the work aspect of the job rather than hazards and risk....We don't say hey when you are down in there watch out for your footing over here, that switch up there is hard to throw, there are two derails up there; and hey, don't forget about that remote zone. As trainmen, we have never really been trained to talk about risk. We are trying to change that and how we identify and train about things."

Conductors felt it was important to discuss risks during job briefs because it informs less experienced individuals of potential hazards and how to identify and avoid them. Conductors who may be less familiar with the territory may benefit from the knowledge of more experienced engineers in identifying potential risks and vice versa. Equally important, the very act of discussing the potential hazards, serves as a form of sensitization and rehearsal, enabling the conductor or engineer to be better prepared. As one conductor stated, "talking about it keeps it on my mind so when I'm down there walking I can look for all of these risks."

3.7   Effects of Lack of Experience on Performance

Athough level of experience is clearly a continuum, the focus of Section 3.6 was on the knowledge and skills exhibited by highly experienced conductors, which we were told can take up to 5 years to develop. In this section, we focus on the other end of the spectrum, relatively new conductors, with minimal OJT (less than a year of experience). We summarize some of the consequences of lack of experience on performance.

Interviews with conductors and trainers suggest that new conductors, who have limited on-the-job experience, are less able to handle situations that require balancing multiple demands on attention. They are less able to effectively problem-solve, plan ahead, or identify and avoid potential safety hazards. Because they have had less first-hand experiences, they are less confident in their knowledge and ability and less likely to catch and correct problems that may arise.

Several of the conductors interviewed indicated that new conductors have "book knowledge" but need more "hands-on" experience to understand how to effectively apply it. New conductors know the mechanics of how to perform specific tasks (e.g., operate a switch, change a knuckle, cut out a car). They also know the operating rules. However, they are less likely to recognize when and how to apply this knowledge. One major consequence of lack of experience is that new conductors are considered less likely to anticipate and take appropriate action to avoid potential hazards. This is partly because they have less familiarity with the territory and therefore do not know what risks it poses. They are also less likely to have developed effective strategies to check for and mitigate risk. As discussed previously, radio communication may also be more challenging for new conductors, likely because they may be less able to handle situations that require balancing multiple demands on attention. It takes more of their attention to listen to, write down, and repeat back authorities. As a consequence, they may have less remaining attentional resources to devote to competing attention demands (e.g., the need to continue to monitor outside the window for upcoming signals). As one conductor described it,

> "Less experienced people get nervous….From time to time they will get so focused on the track warrant that the other duties that are still happening, they might tend to lose focus on them for a bit. It takes experience to get past that. It is really the only thing that will get you past it."

Inexperienced conductors may also be less likely to question the decisions or actions of the locomotive engineer, even in cases where it would be appropriate to do so. This may be because they are less confident in their knowledge (e.g., they may not be sure how long it takes to stop the train) and thus less willing to "second guess" a more experienced locomotive engineer. As one conductor indicated,

> "I know how long it's going to take to stop that train, a young conductor might wait until the last minute to pull the emergency brake application or to say something to [the] engineer, and it might be too late. I'm an experienced conductor. I'm not going to ask. I'm going to reach over and pull it myself. A younger conductor might not because he's worried about the consequences. What that engineer is going to say."

3.8   Training

As part of the RSIA, railroads were required to create a formal program for certifying conductors, including a formal process for training and subsequently assessing competence. In response, the Railroad Safety Advisory Committee (RSAC) had established a Conductor Certification Working Group (which met throughout the course of the CTA) and issued a final rule on November 9, 2011, effective January 1, 2012. As part of the CTA, researchers sought to uncover the current training practices and trends to help identify future training needs and to inform the RSAC group to the extent possible. Interviews with conductors and conductor trainers at various railroads and training programs revealed that there were no standard practices with regard to conductor training. The training practices current at the time of the CTA are described below.

3.8.1 Current Practices

Conductors typically receive training from the railroad by which they are employed. Community colleges also offer conductor training programs. They can serve as a preliminary introduction to railroading; however, most railroads still require conductors to go through the railroad's training courses prior to beginning work. A comprehensive survey of all conductor training programs in the industry was not possible due to time and budget limitations; however, interviews with experienced conductors, directors of conductor training and/or training instructors at two Class I railroads (UP and CSX), and one community college (National Academy of Railroad Sciences, a collaborative partnership between Johnson County Community College and BNSF) revealed that conductor training programs vary significantly in length and scope.

All railroad training programs include a mixture of classroom and OJT and range from approximately 12 to 28 weeks. The length of training varies depending on the railroad's training program and the territory the conductor will operate over. Community college conductor training is typically shorter, lasting on average between 5 and 6 weeks, and many do not offer an OJT component, although they may conduct some training in a yard environment. Presumably because of the variance among conductor training programs, and because railroads have different operating rules, many railroads require new hires to complete their own training, regardless of already having completed a different conductor training program in the past.

Everyone interviewed stressed the importance of training, especially OJT that provides a broad range of relevant experience. OJT gives new hires the opportunity to apply knowledge learned in the classroom out in the field under the supervision of an experienced conductor. Length and scope of OJT across railroads vary, but it is standard practice that training coordinators (associated with the unions) pair new hires with craft instructors for the OJT portion of training. Many conductors noted that the quality of OJT is dependent on the craft instructor, a "seasoned" conductor. Craft instructors are not trained to instruct, and as a consequence, the quality of OJT may differ among new hires even within the same railroad on the same territory. Good craft instructors make an effort to teach new hires and explain their thought processes and the reasons their behind actions over the road so that new hires understand how and why things are done. Conductors mentioned that although training coordinators may try to pair new hires with effective craft instructors, this is not always possible because of schedules and availability. Furthermore, particularly in small yards, there may not be enough experienced conductors who are able to work as craft instructors, and as such, conductors with only 1 or 2 years' experience may act as craft instructors. To provide quality OJT, conductors and conductor trainers both stressed the importance of pairing new hires with competent, highly skilled craft instructors.

Although the quality of OJT depends in large part on the craft instructor, the quantity of OJT that new hires receive depends on the railroad and territory they are assigned to work on. In the yard, conductors learn the basics of railroading, including how to handle equipment, set out cars, and make up trains (especially important when dealing with hazmat). On the mainline, conductors learn over the road tasks such as throwing switches and setting out cars at industry sidings. The longer the OJT is, the more opportunities the conductor has to be exposed to unanticipated incidents, such as broken knuckles or drawbars and watch as the experienced conductor handles these events.

Several conductor training instructors also noted the importance of 'territory specific' training, or familiarization trips. Provided by some railroads, familiarization trips give conductors the opportunity to learn the territory they will be operating over before they begin working the route.

This gives new hires the opportunity to understand things like track curvature and grade, location of signals, detectors and crossings, where to stop the train to avoid blocking crossings, industry layout, and environmental hazards along the track, among others. Territory specific training is especially helpful for conductors who operate over more complex terrain, such as mountain grade territory.

3.8.2 Training Trends

At the time of the CTA, UP was designing a proficiency-based training model. The model, still in its conceptual stages, was designed to alternate classroom training with OJT segments. Under this model students spend time in the classroom learning, go out in the field to apply what they learned, and then potentially return to the classroom to be tested. That cycle would then be repeated until classroom training was complete. This was designed to shorten training so that, for example, conductors who will work in a yard strictly loading and unloading coal trains won't need to spend time in the classroom and in the field receiving Remote Control Locomotive (RCL) training. In addition, this training model would allow the railroad to determine early on who, from the training applicants, are fit for the job, rather than take them through classroom training only to find that they cannot satisfactorily apply what they learned in the field.

In addition to operational and rules training, railroads have also begun training employees to be assertive and say something when an unsafe behavior or shortcut is observed. The generic term for this training is CRM. CRM is the optimization of the person-machine interface and the interpersonal activities of the crew. CRM training focuses on interpersonal skills and crew communication, with the goal of having the crew function optimally as a team. Training instructors noted that this type of training is very important for conductors, especially new hires. Several conductors expressed that, as new hires, they may have felt intimidated telling experienced "old-head" engineers when they are engaging in unsafe behaviors or shortcuts. Other conductors mentioned hesitation to pull the emergency brake when they saw that the train was going toward an overspeed because that might appear as undermining the engineer.

At the time this report was written, UP had implemented a "Total Safety Culture" approach in several yards. Total Safety Culture (TSC) is a voluntary peer-based observation system that encourages peers to coach one another and discuss unsafe behaviors as they occur. TSC gives workers the opportunity to talk about their own, or others', unsafe behaviors without fear of punitive punishment. If a railroad employee sees another employee engaging in unsafe behaviors, the employee will point it out. The employees then have the opportunity to discuss the unsafe behaviors and how to avoid them in the future. This might involve going back to the railroad and pointing to specific tasks or equipment that necessitate unsafe behavior by design. There is an option at that time to do an anonymous writeup about the unsafe behavior but only with the employee's permission. That data is analyzed by members of the I-Team (TSC employees) who then take action to mitigate opportunities for unsafe behavior and teach courses to correct the behavior.

TSC employees are made up of trainmen who are chosen jointly by the union and railroad. Employees rotate out of their TSC positions every 1-2 years to allow as many employees as possible to participate and so that no TSC employee is seen as a "management type." Some work full time as TSC employees for their tenure, others continue to work as trainmen.

3.8.3 Training Needs and Conductor Certification

Interviews were also intended to uncover opinions regarding the need for conductor certification and potential room for improvement in current conductor training practices.

Individuals we interviewed indicated that conductor certification was important for two reasons: (1) to establish a uniform standard of training and (2) to ensure conductors meet health and physical requirements. Conductor certification (49 CFR Part 242, Docket No. FRA-2009-0035), as mandated by RSIA and defined through the RSAC process, requires railroads to have a formal program for certifying conductors. Similar to engineer certification, this rule requires railroads to have a formal process for training prospective conductors and determining their competency prior to allowing them to work.

With regard to a uniform standard of training, interview participants agreed that although conductors received adequate time in the classroom learning the rules, more OJT was needed to apply them. A majority of the conductors we interviewed also expressed a desire to standardize OJT so that guidelines exist for specific situations and events that all conductor trainees must experience. Territory familiarization training is also important but should not come at the expense of OJT and is not necessary for conductor certification. Rather, familiarization trips should be given after conductors are certified and before they begin work over an unfamiliar route.

Currently, jobs are assigned based on seniority, which typically results in new hires having the least desirable, riskiest jobs. Several conductors indicated that the old procedure of starting new hires as brakemen/switchmen before becoming conductors allowed new hires to learn valuable skills in the yard prior to working on the mainline. New hires would work for a year as brakemen/switchmen, giving them time to work with yardmasters and other workers in the yard, to acquire skills and experience, and to learn the basics of railroading and how to handle equipment before they begin working on the mainline alongside an engineer. Today, the positions of switchmen/brakemen do not exist in the same quantity, so this is no longer the path new hires go through; however, the main point to draw from the feedback is that there may be a need to compensate for this loss of hands on experience early on in the conductor's career.

Experienced conductors and training instructors also indicated the need to train for rare but serious events and incidents. When possible, conductors should receive hands-on experience dealing with these incidents (perhaps in a simulated environment), especially for events that conductors are unlikely to experience during OJT. Many conductors gave the example of learning to repair a broken knuckle. Learning about broken knuckles in the classroom is very different from physically picking up a 75-pound knuckle in the field. Conductors operating over mountain grade territory reiterated this need. One conductor operating in mountain grade territory noted that learning about tying hand brakes in the classroom is much different than doing so in the field. The conductor noted that on flat terrain and in good weather, tying hand brakes is neither cognitively nor physically very challenging. However, for a 14,000-ton loaded grain train with 100 cars on a 2-percent grade, the conductor would need to tie 60 hand brakes. In 2 feet of snow and difficult walking conditions, tying 60 hand brakes is no small feat and could take several hours. However when learning about tying hand brakes in the classroom, one may not realize this. In his words:

"If it's a nice spring day, if you [tied all 60 handbrakes] in an hour that would be really, really fast. It typically takes a couple hours—if it's a nice day. But, for example, you could have 2 feet of snow out there. And it depends on walking conditions. We don't have roads in this area that run alongside of the tracks, so walking is difficult, even without snow."

Experienced conductors and training instructors also stressed the importance of training so that tasks become automated and reflexive and perhaps more so in mountain grade territory where there is less margin for error. One conductor operating over mountain grade territory gave the example of the 5-mile overspeed rule. If a new hire had to find said rule, by the time the rule was found the train would likely be 10 or 15 miles overspeed and it would be too late.

Many conductors mentioned the need to train new hires to anticipate and discuss risk. Currently, conductors and engineers are required to conduct job briefings at the start of each run to discuss work planned for the run, but many conductors stressed the importance of discussing risk factors for the route continuously during the trip. Continuous job briefings about the route are especially important for new hires because they give the locomotive engineer opportunities to remind the conductor about upcoming events and associated risks.

Similarly, experienced conductors noted the importance of providing CRM training to give new hires the confidence to tell experienced engineers when they are taking shortcuts, engaging in unsafe behavior, or not following operating rules. One conductor discussed this at length, especially with regard to overspeeds in mountain grade territory. Because of the steep grade, trains can gain speed extremely quickly, so if the locomotive engineer is even approaching the maximum allowable speed, the conductor should feel comfortable calling it out instead of assuming the engineer will slow down the train. An inexperienced conductor may feel foolish doing so, particularly if working with an experienced locomotive engineer who has worked in mountain grade territory and knows the rules, but this communication is important, and a good locomotive engineer would appreciate the callout.

With regard to health and physical requirements, conductors did not have specific suggestions for conductor certification, although most believed that the final rule with regard to health and physical requirements will be similar to the those found in Part 240 of Title 49 of the Code of Federal Regulations (49 CFR Part 240) for locomotive engineer certification.

4.   Summary and Conclusions

This cognitive task analysis examined the cognitive and collaborative demands placed on conductors and the knowledge and skills that experienced conductors have developed that enable them to operate safely and efficiently. The study uncovered a variety of domain knowledge and skills that distinguish experienced conductors from less experienced ones. Conductors develop experience over time through repeated practice on routine tasks (e.g., communicating over the radio) as well as first-hand experience with relatively rare situations (e.g., the need to troubleshoot a train malfunction).

In this section, we summarize some of the key findings of the study and discuss their implications for two emerging issues: (1) the role of conductors as new PTC technology is introduced; and (2) conductor training. Finally, we conclude the report with future research needs stemming from our findings.

4.1   Conductors and Locomotive Engineers as a Joint Cognitive System

Conductors and locomotive engineers operate as a tightly coupled cooperative team. They function as what is referred to as a *joint cognitive system* (Woods and Hollnagel, 2006). Conductors and locomotive engineers jointly contribute to the set of cognitive activities required to operate the train safely and efficiently. Although each has a distinct set of formal responsibilities—the conductor is responsible for managing the train consist and the locomotive engineer is responsible for running the locomotive—in practice, they operate as an integrated team, contributing knowledge and backing each other up as necessary. They not only participate jointly in monitoring outside the window, but also, as described in Section 3, they participate jointly in planning activities, problem-solving, and identifying and mitigating risk.

When operating on the mainline, conductors not only serve as a "second pair of eyes," alerting the locomotive engineer to upcoming signals and potential hazards (e.g., activity at grade crossings; people working on or about the track), they also contribute knowledge and decisionmaking to the locomotive engineer when the crew is faced with challenging situations. Interview participants provided us with many examples where an experienced conductor compensated for knowledge limitations of an inexperienced locomotive engineer. Conductors drew on their knowledge of the territory and range of experiences to support decisions such as when to initiate braking and where to stop to maximize safety and efficiency.

Conductors also serve an important redundant check and backup role, reminding the locomotive engineers of upcoming work zones and speed restrictions. They actively work to ensure that the locomotive engineer remains alert by engaging him or her in conversation. If necessary, they will also pull the emergency brake in cases where the locomotive engineer has not responded quickly (whether because of inattention, lack of knowledge, or incapacitation).

Locomotive engineers serve an important support role for conductors as well. They help to fill in knowledge gaps, support planning, and help conductors anticipate and mitigate risks. Experienced engineers serve an important mentoring role for less experienced conductors and vice versa.

4.2 The Role of Conductors in Handling Unanticipated Situations

In addition to serving as support and backup for the locomotive engineer, another important role that conductors play on the mainline is to handle unanticipated situations. This includes a variety of situations where conductors need to troubleshoot the source of the problem and, if necessary, cut out cars.

As described in Section 3, these unanticipated situations impose cognitive as well as physical demands on the conductor. This includes the need to troubleshoot the source of the problem (e.g., in the case of an alert from a hotbox detector) as well as to determine how to safely handle the situation. Issues that arise include where to safely stop, how many hand brakes to use to secure the train, and how to properly sequence the remaining cars in the consist (e.g., to ensure that hazardous cars are properly placed). As discussed in Section 3, experienced conductors have developed a variety of skills and strategies that enable them to handle these non-routine situations more safely and efficiently. Conductors acquire this knowledge through first-hand experience on the job as well as by working with more experienced conductors and engineers.

4.3 Implications of Results

4.3.1 The Role of Conductors and PTC Technology

One of the questions that motivated the cognitive task analysis was how new technologies, such as PTC, would impact the role of conductors in the future. The cognitive task analysis addresses this issue by laying out the multiple ways in which conductors contribute to safe and efficient train operations and contrasts this with the anticipated features of PTC.

Anticipated features of positive train technology are intended to serve some of the cognitive support functions that conductors currently provide to locomotive engineers. These include providing reminders of upcoming signals, work zones, and speed restrictions to locomotive engineers. It also includes automatically applying emergency brakes to stop the train in cases where the train would otherwise exceed speed limits or limits of track authority. Both of these are functions that conductors currently provide.

As documented in Section 3 and summarized in Section 4.1, conductors provide a number of additional cognitive support functions to locomotive engineers that PTC does not provide. These functions include supporting locomotive engineers in monitoring events outside the cab window for potential obstacles and hazards undetected by automated systems (e.g., people working on or around the track, trespassers, cars at grade crossings). They also include filling knowledge gaps that locomotive engineers may have and supporting decisionmaking. Knowledge and decisionmaking support is especially important in the case of less experienced locomotive engineers. Conductors also serve an important role in handling unanticipated events and keeping the locomotive engineer alert, especially on long monotonous trips where there is a risk of falling asleep.

Presently, PTC has not been implemented on all applicable rail lines; therefore, how PTC will change cab operations, for example, crew coordination, is still an open question. Although PTC will be installed as an overlay system—therefore not materially changing the train crew's roles

43

and responsibilities—conductors and locomotive engineers interviewed brought up the question of whether PTC will bring about one-person operations in the future.

Findings from this CTA indicate that PTC will not account for all of the cognitive support functions the conductor currently provides. Therefore, if industry seeks to implement one-person operations in the future, it would be important to first compile a detailed list of the physical and cognitive tasks both the engineer and conductor perform in the cab, determine which of these tasks PTC will account for, and understand how the locomotive engineer's responsibilities would change in a one-person operation. For example, will additional tasks and responsibilities be placed upon the engineer? A subsequent job and cognitive task analysis would identify any new knowledge, skills and abilities required by the locomotive engineer as well as new cognitive demands placed on the locomotive engineer. A related issue conductors mentioned in interviews is that conductors typically move on to become locomotive engineers, so time spent as a conductor serves a training function. If one-person operations became commonplace, this would no longer be the case, and incoming locomotive engineers will have spent less time working alongside an engineer and could come into the engineer's role at a less experienced level. In that case, it is important to consider the safety implications of that situation and how to counteract those with training.

4.3.2 Potential to Accelerate Development of Expertise

The results of the cognitive task analysis provide multiple illustrations of the value of experience in the field for consolidating knowledge, developing skill, and building confidence. Conductors stressed the importance of gaining experience with the territory, having opportunities to practice routine skills such as communicating over the radio so that they require less focused attention, and having direct hands-on experience performing tasks that may arise rarely but are critical from a safety perspective (e.g., handling train malfunctions).

The results suggest an opportunity to potentially accelerate building conductor expertise by providing a broader set of carefully selected experiences as part of OJT. These would enable new conductors to more quickly build their knowledge of the territory and direct experience with a variety of situations. The conductors and training instructors we interviewed consistently stressed the importance of OJT and the need to consider more and better integrated OJT to build conductor expertise more quickly.

The results also point to the importance of teaching conductors and locomotive engineers effective cab communication and job briefing skills. Interviews with conductors and trainers suggest that these communication skills are not always explicitly taught and not sufficiently stressed during training. Morgan et al. (2006) note that positive safety benefits, including improved communication and teamwork among crewmembers, conflict resolution, and maintaining situational awareness, have been shown to increase as a result of formal training in core CRM. More focus on effective communication and increased CRM training would enhance teamwork. It would encourage joint problem-solving and decisionmaking that leverages the knowledge and skills of the entire train crew for safer and more efficient performance.

Finally, the results of the cognitive task analysis point to the value of carefully pairing conductors and locomotive engineers so that less experienced individuals are paired with more experienced ones. This provides opportunities for knowledge transfer between crewmembers, further accelerating development of expertise.

4.4   Open Questions and Future Research Needs

Although the cognitive task analysis provided insight to freight conductor work, it also raised additional questions surrounding conductor expertise, conductor training, and conductor certification. Future research is required to answer these, and other, questions that will surely arise in the coming years as a result of new technology, operating rules, and certification requirements.

4.4.1 The Expertise Continuum

This report describes the end points of expertise ("inexperienced" versus highly experienced), but we know expertise is a continuum. With that in mind, the following are open questions related to level of train crew expertise and safety enhancement:

- Is there evidence that less experienced conductors (and engineers) are more vulnerable to certain kinds of risk (to themselves and to others)? It should be possible to address this question by examining industry databases (e.g. the near-miss database or other accident databases).

- If less experienced crewmembers are more at risk, what can we do to protect them more effectively?

- How do you know that someone is trained adequately to handle the situations they are placed in? Would it be helpful to assess train crewmembers annually, for example, to measure the skills acquired during that time?

- Similarly, is there a way to gradually phase in what types of assignments they are given to ensure they are not placed in a situation they are not prepared for? Is there a way to identify systematically what kinds of tasks they can be given and which should be avoided until they receive more training and/or experience in the field?

- A related question assesses the adequacy of territory knowledge as individuals are moved to a new territory. Is there a way to assess that they have sufficiently mastered the territory before allowing them to go "on their own?" What risk controls are needed when conductors change territories so that they are protected from unfamiliar hazards?

- Is there a way to ensure that conductors and locomotive engineers are paired up systematically so that at least one of them is familiar with the territory they are about to travel on as well as the job they are being asked to perform? One of the problems is that inexperienced people "don't know what they don't know'" and therefore cannot anticipate the risk and challenges and cannot prepare for them. Pairing a conductor and locomotive engineer so that at least one of them is highly experienced can mitigate that problem.

4.4.2 Opportunities to Enhance Training

A significant finding of the cognitive task analysis, discussed in Section 3.8, is that on-the-job training is important for helping conductors translate classroom knowledge to real-life skills. In Section 4.3.2, we suggest that additional targeted OJT may accelerate building conductor expertise. Future research on how the railroad industry might enhance OJT may help the railroads develop more effective OJT. One question to ask is how do other (successful) industries structure their OJT to get new hires up to speed effectively? This may provide a roadmap for how the railroad industry can enhance OJT without conducting a formal assessment.

In addition to OJT, our results clearly indicate that a need for CRM training. Interviews with conductor training instructors revealed a growing recognition of the importance of CRM among practitioners, and we saw elements of CRM beginning to be taught. How can we enhance CRM training and ensure this translates into good crew communication in the field? Our results clearly indicate that CRM is especially important in the case of an inexperienced crewmember paired with a highly experienced crewmember, where the inexperienced crewmember may not feel comfortable speaking up about a particular situation for fear of being wrong or believing that the experienced crewmember must know best. However, as we suggest in the previous section, pairing inexperienced crewmembers with experienced ones is important for knowledge transfer and train safety.

4.4.3 Implications of Certification

A final open question surrounds the implications of conductor certification on the industry. What level of expertise does conductor certification imply? In Section 4.4.1, questions are raised surrounding a conductor's level of experience and the work he should be allowed to do. Does certification mean that a less experienced conductor will be expected to have the same knowledge as a highly experienced conductor? How will the railroads distinguish between certification and experience level and assign employees accordingly?

4.4.4 Future Research Needs

The cognitive task analysis identified the knowledge and skills required of expert conductors at a high level. Additional studies can be performed to examine the cognitive skills at a more detailed level and to answer the open-ended questions posed in the previous sections. Field studies, for example, can be performed by using head and eye tracking devices or video recordings to understand conductor processes in more detail.

In addition, although this report focused on systematic classroom and field training, simulator studies and simulator training are useful tools as well. Simulator studies might provide a more practical means of researching issues surrounding expertise level, CRM, and the impact of PTC on railroad operations. Future simulator research could include studies to:

- explore how skills expand with level of expertise (e.g., studies that look at the ability to multitask, communicate effectively with crewmembers, identify risks, monitor out the window, etc., across conductors with varying skill levels)

- explore issues in CRM (e.g., studies to uncover problems in team processes that suggest the need for CRM and a follow-on study to understand the impact of CRM training)

- explore introduction of PTC displays on crew cognitive and collaborative processes

5.   References

Bisantz, A., and Roth, E. M. (2008). Analysis of Cognitive Work. In Deborah A. Boehm-Davis (Ed.) *Reviews of Human Factors and Ergonomics Volume 3*. Santa Monica, CA: Human Factors and Ergonomics Society. 1-43.

Crandall, B., Klein, G., and Hoffman, R. R. (2006). *Working Minds: A Practitioner's Guide to Cognitive Task Analysis,* Cambridge, MA: The MIT Press.

Frings, D. (2011). The effects of group monitoring on fatigue-related einstellung during mathematical problem solving. *Journal of Experimental Psychology: Applied* 17(4), 371-381.

Huey, B. M., and Wickens, C. D. (1993). Workload Transitions: Implications for Individual and Team Performance. Washington, DC: National Academy Press.

Morgan, C. M., Olson, L. E., Kyte, T. B., Roop, S. S., and Carlisle, T. D. (2006). Railroad Crew Resource Management (CRM): Survey of Teams in the Railroad Operating Environment and Identification of Available CRM Training Method. Washington, D. C.: U. S. Department of Transportation/Federal Railroad Administration (DOT/FRA/ORD-06/10). Retrieved from http://www.fra.dot.gov/downloads/research/ord0610.pdf.

Patterson, E. S., Roth, E. M., and Woods, D. D. (2010). Facets of complexity in situated work. In E. S. Patterson and J. Miller (Eds.) *Macrocognition Metrics and Scenarios: Design and Evaluation for Real-World Teams*. Ashgate Publishing. ISBN 978-0-7546-7578-5.

Potter, S. S., Roth, E. M., Woods, D., and Elm, W. C. (2000). Bootstrapping multiple converging cognitive task analysis techniques for system design. In J. M. Schraagen, S. F. Chipman, and V. L. Shalin (Eds.), *Cognitive Task Analysis*. Mahwah, NJ: Erlbaum.

Qualification and Certification of Locomotive Engineers, 49 C.F.R § 240.

Qualification and Certification of Conductors, 49 C.F.R. § 242.

Roth, E. M. (2008). Uncovering the Requirements of Cognitive Work. *Human Factors*, 50 (3), 475-480. (Golden Anniversary Special Section on Discoveries and Developments). Retrieved from http://www.ingentaconnect.com/content/hfes/hf/2008/00000050/00000003/art00022.

Roth, E. M. (2009). Understanding Cognitive Strategies for Shared Situation Awareness Across a Distributed System: An Example of Strategies Analysis. In A. M. Bisantz and C. M. Burns (Eds) *Applications of Cognitive Work Analysis*. Boca Raton, FL: CRC Press, Taylor & Francis Group, pp. 129–147.

Roth, E. M., Malsch, N., and Multer, J. (2001). Understanding how train dispatchers manage and control trains: Results of a cognitive task analysis. Washington, D. C.: U. S. Department of Transportation/Federal Railroad Administration. (DOT/FRA/ORD-01/02) Retrieved from http://www.fra.dot.gov/downloads/Research/ord0102.pdf.

Roth, E. M., Multer, J., and Raslear, T. (2006). Shared situation awareness as a contributor to high reliability performance in railroad operations. *Organization Studies*, 27(7), 967-987.

Roth, E., and Multer, J. (2007). Communication and Coordination Demands of Railroad Roadway Worker Activities and Implications for New Technology. Washington, D.C.: U.S. Department of Transportation/Federal Railroad Administration (DOT/FRA/ORD-07/28) Retrieved from http://www.fra.dot.gov/downloads/Research/ord0728.pdf.

Roth, E. M., and Multer, J. (2009). Technology Implications of a Cognitive Task Analysis for Locomotive Engineers. Washington, D.C.: U.S. Department of Transportation/Federal Railroad Administration (DOT/FRA/ORD-09/03) Retrieved from http://www.fra.dot.gov/downloads/Research/ord0903.pdf.

Roth, E. M., Multer, J., and Scott, R. (2009). Understanding and contributing to resilient work systems. In Nemeth, C. P., Hollnagel, E., and Dekker, S. (Eds.), *Resilience Engineering Perspectives Volume 2: Preparation and Restoration.* Burlington, VT: Ashgate Publishing Company.

Salas, E., Diazgranodos, D., and Lazzara, E. (2011 Dec.). Promoting teamwork when lives depend on it: What Matters in the Railroad Industry. *Transportation Research Circular*, Number E-C159.

Salas, E. E., Sims, D. E., and Burke, C. S. (2005). Is there a 'big five' in teamwork? *Small Group Research*, 36, 555-599.

Sanders, M. S., Jankovich, J. J., and Goodpaster, P. R. (1974). *Task Analysis for the Jobs of Train Conductor and Brakeman*: Naval Ammunition Depot Crane Ind.

Schraagen, J. M., Chipman, S. F., and Shalin, V. L. (Eds.). (2000). *Cognitive Task Analysis.* Mahwah, NJ: Lawrence Erlbaum Associates.

Schneider, W. and Shiffrin R. M. (1977). Controlled and automatic human information processing I: Detection, serch and attention. *Psychological Review*, 84, 1-66.

Walsh, B., Golay, L., Barnes-Farrell, J., and Morrow, S. (2010). A Job Analysis Design for the Rail Industry: Description and model analysis of the job of freight conductor. (IPAC TR-2010-01). Prepared for the Federal Railroad Administration and the Volpe National Transportation Research Center. Storrs, CT: University of Connecticut, Industrial Psychology Applications Center.

Woods, D.D. and Hollnagel, E. (2006). Joint Cognitive Systems: Patterns in Cognitive Systems Engineering. Boca Raton, FL: CRC Press.

Wreathall, J., Woods, D. D., Bing, A. J. and Christoffersen, K. (2007). Relative Risk of Workload Transitions in Positive Train Control. Washington D.C.: U. S. Department of Transportation/Federal Railroad Administration (DOT/FRA/ORD-07/12) Retrieved from http://www.fra.dot.gov/downloads/Research/ord0712.pdf.

APPENDIX A. STAKEHOLDER INTERVIEW QUESTIONS

Range of Conductor Roles and Responsibilities:

In trying to define and bound the scope of the Conductor CTA we are trying to understand the differences in conductor roles and responsibilities and the kinds of issues that arise in different types of railroad operations:

Passenger vs. Freight Operations:

- What are the major differences in the roles of Conductors in Passenger vs. Freight? What are the core commonalities?
- Are there different issues or concerns that are emerging in relation to certification of new conductors in Passenger vs. Freight?
- Are there different issues or concerns that are emerging in relation to emerging technologies and their impact on the roles and responsibilities of conductors in Passenger vs. Freight operations?
- Are there any other new emerging issues or concerns associated with Passenger vs. Freight Operations we should be aware of?

Mainline vs. Yard Switching Operations

- What are the major differences in the roles of Conductors in Mainline vs. Yard Switching Operations? What are the core commonalities?
- Do Conductors specialize in Mainline or Yard operations or do they routinely switch between the two?
- Are there different issues or concerns that are emerging in relation to certification of new conductors in Mainline vs. Yard operation?
- Are there different issues or concerns that are emerging in relation to emerging technologies and their impact on the roles and responsibilities of conductors in Mainline vs. Yard operations?
- Are there any other new emerging issues or concerns associated with Mainline vs. Yard Operations we should be aware of?

Are there other distinctions among types of conductors we should be aware of?

Emerging Technologies and their Impact on Role of Conductors:

There are a number of new technologies that are currently under development that are likely to affect the role of conductors. These include new track switching technologies that may reduce the need for conductors to manually switch track position. It also includes new train control technologies (e.g., Positive Train Control technologies) that may alter the cognitive and communication demands on the train crew.

- What railroads are working on systems that are likely to impact the role of conductors – both physical activities (e.g., switch operations) and mental activities (e.g., communicating and coordinating with the Locomotive Engineer)?
- How do you see these technologies impacting/changing the role of Conductors? Their training requirements?
- What new issues/concerns do you see arising with the introduction of these technologies as they relate to the role of and demands on Conductors?
- Are there other emerging technologies in addition to PTC and track switching technologies that you see impacting Conductor roles and responsibilities?
- Is there any information that we could collect during interviews/focus groups of conductors that could help inform these issues?

Conductor Certification

A railroad safety advisory committee task force is being convened to develop regulations for certification of railroad conductors. We understand that this issue was initiated by UTU. We are trying to understand what is motivating the need for conductor certification, and what information we might be able to collect to could inform development of certification requirements.

- Can you give us your perspective on the need for certifying conductors?
- Are the certification requirements likely to be different for different types of Conductors (e.g., Passenger vs. Freight; Yard vs. Mainline)?
- How are conductors being trained today and what do you see as some of the shortfalls?
- Have there been incidents that have been attributed to gaps in knowledge or skill of new conductors?
- What do you see as the kinds of knowledge or skill that new conductors need to develop to perform the duties expected of them?
- What types of errors are new conductors vulnerable to that may put them at risk of an accident?
- What railroads are taking the lead in developing more effective training programs? Defining certification requirements?
- What do you see as some of the open questions/issues that need to be addressed in support of developing regulations for certification of railroad conductors?
- Is there any information that we could collect during interviews/focus groups with conductors that could help inform these issues?

Recommendations for Scope and Focus of CTA:

We initially thought to focus CTA efforts on the role of Freight Conductors in mainline operations.
- Given the emerging issues should we be shifting or expanding our focus?

Recommendations for Railroad/Stakeholder Contacts:

- Do you have recommendations for railroad/sites to visit to conduct focus groups with conductors/locomotive engineers?
- Do you have recommendations for individuals to contact to help arrange these visits?
- Do you have any recommendations for additional individuals or stakeholder groups that it might be useful to interview prior to setting up focus group visits?

Conductor Training Interview Questions (NARS)

- Can you tell us a little bit about the conductor training program at NARS?
    - How long is it, what does it covered? (Is there any training materials we can obtain, syllabus?)
    - Does the conductor training program cover both mainline and yard operations?
    - How does the NARS training program differ from other conductor training programs (other railroads)?
- Once conductors complete the program, is there an apprenticeship program?
- What types of knowledge and skills do you feel can only be learned on the job?
- What is the career path for a conductor?
    - where they are drawn from?
    - Do Conductors specialize in Mainline or Yard operations or do they routinely switch between the two?
    - Do they tend to become Loc Engineers?
    - How long do they stay as Conductor before switching to other positions?
- In your opinion, how long does it typically take to become an 'expert'/seasoned/fully competent and confident conductor?

Conductor Training Interview Questions (UP and CSX)

Can you tell us a little bit about the conductor training program at ___ (UP/CSX)?
- Generally, what is the demographic of the new hires?
    - People off the street/no rail background?
    - Students who have gone through other RR training courses, such as NARS?
    - Are prior conductors (from other railroads) required to go through training?
- How long is training?
- Does the conductor training program cover both mainline and yard operations?
- What does it cover?
    - (any training materials we can obtain, syllabus?)

- Can you tell us a little bit about OJT?
    - How long is the OJT portion?
    - What does OJT cover?
    - Are there standard for how this training takes place or does each mentor decide what to focus on?
        - What must every conductor experience during OJT? (e.g. replacing a knuckle, detecting hot journals, etc.)
    - What types of knowledge and skills do you feel can only be learned on the job?
    - How much of OJT is rail yard location specific?

- Craft Instructors?
    - How are craft instructors matched with new hires?
        - What are the craft instructors' backgrounds?
        - Do they receive craft instructor training?
    - How many craft instructors are typically at each rail yard?
    - Do new hires have the same craft instructors each time?

- How are new hires evaluated?

- How do you assess competency or knowledge acquired during training?
    - Classroom evaluation versus OJT evaluation?
    - (are there evaluation forms we can obtain?)
- At the conclusion of training, how do you establish that a conductor has the skills required to do their work safely and properly?
- Are there performance standards that a conductor must demonstrate before working in the field? (checklist we can obtain?)

- 'Expert' Conductors
    - In your opinion, how long does it typically take to become an 'expert'/seasoned/fully competent and confident conductor?
    - Is there an apprenticeship or probationary period for new hires after they have completed training?

- Conductor Certification

A railroad safety advisory committee task force is being convened to develop regulations for certification of railroad conductors.

- Can you give us your perspective on the need for certifying conductors?
- What knowledge and skill do you feel is critical for conductors to possess that need to be included in a certification program?
- Do you feel an apprenticeship (OJT) portion should be included?
- Have there been incidents that have been attributed to gaps in knowledge or skill of new conductors?
- Do you know of situations where conductors are placed in jobs for which they are not prepared?

Questions for Conductor Training Instructors

Opening Question:

Can you tell us a little about your railroad background.

Cognitive and Collaborative Demands *(30 – 45 minutes)*

We are interested in understanding the knowledge and skills that it takes to be a competent and confident conductor – and particularly the knowledge, skills and strategies that it takes to handle the real complexities that can arise during train runs.

Let's go through each of the major 'roles' of a conductor as we understand them and ask you to tell us what are the main activities involved, what the real challenges are, and what knowledge and skills experienced conductors have developed to meet those challenges.

We are particularly interested in what are the real challenges that arise in the field that require *knowledge and skills beyond what is covered in 'training manuals' and 'operating rules' -- 'undocumented' skills of the craft.* As we go through these questions we'll be trying to get examples of specific situations that have recently occurred that illustrate your points.

1. One role of conductors relates to being in charge of the train consist (supervising the operation and conduct of the train)
    *   Can you briefly describe what this involves?
    *   Can you tell us about some of the complications that can arise to make this task hard (challenging)?
        *   Can you give us a recent example that illustrates your point?
    *   Are there differences between how an experienced and an inexperienced person might handle the situation?
        *   What are typical 'pitfalls'/mistakes that a less experienced person might make?

2. Another role of the conductor is to communicate with, support, and serve as a backup to the Locomotive Engineer (alerting him or her) of upcoming speed restrictions, workzones, etc.
    *   Can you briefly describe what this involves?
    *   Under what circumstances is it particularly important for the Conductor to serve this support/backup function? What are the types of situations where the Locomotive Engineer really needs the conductor's help?
        *   Can you give me a recent example that illustrates your point?
    *   Are there differences between how an experienced and an inexperienced conductor might handle the situation?
        *   What are typical 'pitfalls'/mistakes that a less experienced person might make?

    *   Are there other situations where the Conductor and Loc. Engineer need to coordinate closely?
        *   Can you give me a recent example that illustrates your point?

3. Conductors are also responsible for communicating with other railroad personnel
    *   Who besides the loc engineer is the conductor required to communicate/coordinate with?
    *   Can you tell us about some of the complications that can arise to make this task hard (challenging)?
        *   Can you give me a recent example that illustrates your point?

- Are there differences between how an experienced and an inexperienced person might handle the situation?
- What are typical 'pitfalls'/mistakes that a less experienced person might make?

- Besides the 'formal' requirements for communication and coordination, are there other situations where conductors will communicate/coordinate with other railroad personnel – informal communication or work practices that improve safety or help train operations run more smoothly (e.g., letting roadway workers know that a train is coming in the other direction... things that are thought of as 'courtesies' but that are actually important to safety)?

4. A fourth role relates to detecting, troubleshooting and responding to equipment malfunctions
    - Can you briefly describe what this involves?
    - Can you tell me about some of the complications that can arise to make this task hard (challenging)?
        - Can you give me a recent example that illustrates your point?
    - Are there differences between how an experienced and an inexperienced person might handle the situation?
        - What are typical 'pitfalls'/mistakes that a less experienced person might make?

5. Another role relates to handling non-routine/unanticipated/unplanned for situations
    - Can you give me some examples of some of the kinds of unexpected/unplanned for situations that can arise enroute? (e.g., train malfunction, obstacle on track, hazardous spill)
        - What is the role of the conductor in these situations?
        - What makes these situations challenging?
        - What knowledge and skills are required to handle these types of situations?
        - Are there differences between how an experienced and an inexperienced person might handle the situation?
            - What are typical 'pitfalls'/mistakes that a less experienced person might make?

6. Are there other major roles or responsibilities that I haven't mentioned (other than completing and maintaining required records and forms)?

7. Are there other informal work practices (that go beyond what is covered in formal written policies, rule-books and procedures) that experienced conductors engage in that improve efficiency and safety?

Emerging Technologies and their Impact on Role of Conductors (30 minute)

There are a number of new technologies that are currently under development that are likely to affect the role of conductors. These include new track switching technologies that may reduce the need for conductors to manually switch track position. It also includes new train control technologies (e.g., Positive Train Control technologies) that may alter the cognitive and communication demands on the train crew.

- How do you see these technologies impacting/changing the role of Conductors? Their training requirements?
- In particular how do you see PTC impacting the role of conductors?
    - Handout on PTC
- How do you see PTC impacting requirements for Conductor training requirements?

- Under what train operating conditions do you feel it would be possible to have one person operation? For example are there certain types of train territory where one person operation would be no problem?
- Under what train operating conditions is it critical to have two people in the cab?

- If a railroad went to one person operation what activities would need to be taken over by Loc. Engineer or by an 'aiding systems'?
- What functions that are currently being done by conductors do you feel would no longer be well supported or would need to be done differently?
- What new issues/concerns do you see arising with the introduction of these technologies as they relate to the role of and demands on Conductors?

Conductor Certification (15 minutes)

A railroad safety advisory committee task force is being convened to develop regulations for certification of railroad conductors.

- Can you give us your perspective on the need for certifying conductors?
- What knowledge and skill do you feel is critical for conductors to possess that need to be included in a certification program?
- Do you feel an apprenticeship portion should be included?
    - Have there been incidents that have been attributed to gaps in knowledge or skill of new conductors?

Questions for Freight Conductors & Locomotive Engineers

Opening Question:

Can you tell us a little about your railroad background.

Cognitive and Collaborative Demands

Let's go through each of the major 'roles' of a conductor as we understand them and ask you to tell us what are the main activities involved, what the real challenges are, and what knowledge and skills experienced conductors have developed to meet those challenges.

We are particularly interested in what are the real challenges that arise in the field that require *knowledge and skills beyond what is covered in 'training manuals' and 'operating rules' -- 'undocumented' skills of the craft*. As we go through these questions we'll be trying to get examples of specific situations that have recently occurred that illustrate your points.

(Approximately 10 minutes per topic)

8. One role of conductors relates to being in charge of the train (supervising the safe operation and conduct of the train – managing the train consist and managing the related paper work)
    * Can you briefly describe what this involves? What specific tasks are involved?
    * Which of these tasks would you say are the most mentally challenging or error-prone?
    * Can you tell us about some of the complications that can arise to make this task hard (challenging)?
        * Can you give us a recent example that illustrates your point?
    * Are there differences between how an experienced and an inexperienced person might handle the situation?
        * What are typical 'pitfalls'/mistakes that a less experienced person might make that a more experienced person has learned to avoid?

9. Another role of the conductor is to communicate with, support, and serve as a backup to the Locomotive Engineer (alerting him or her) of upcoming speed restrictions, workzones, etc. (and other crew members if applicable).
    * Can you briefly describe what this involves?
    * Which of these tasks would you say are the most mentally challenging or error-prone?
    * Can you tell us about some of the complications that can arise to make this task hard (challenging)?
        * Can you give us a recent example that illustrates your point?
    * Are there differences between how an experienced and an inexperienced person might handle the situation?
        * What are typical 'pitfalls'/mistakes that a less experienced person might make that a more experienced person has learned to avoid?

    * Under what circumstances is it particularly important for the Conductor to serve this support/backup function? What are the types of situations where the Locomotive Engineer really needs the conductor's help?
        * Can you give me a recent example that illustrates your point?

10. Conductors are also responsible for communicating with other railroad personnel
    * Who besides the loc engineer is the conductor required to communicate/coordinate with?
    * Can you tell us about some of the complications that can arise to make this task hard (challenging)?

- Can you give me a recent example that illustrates your point?
- Are there differences between how an experienced and an inexperienced person might handle the situation?
- What are typical 'pitfalls'/mistakes that a less experienced person might make?

- Besides the 'formal' requirements for communication and coordination, are there other situations where conductors will communicate/coordinate with other railroad personnel – informal communication or work practices that improve safety or help train operations run more smoothly (e.g., letting roadway workers know that a train is coming in the other direction… things that are thought of as 'courtesies' but that are actually important to safety)?

11. Another role relates to handling non-routine/unanticipated/unplanned for situations
    - Can you give me some examples of some of the kinds of unexpected/unplanned for situations that can arise enroute? (e.g., train malfunction, obstacle on track, hazardous spill)
        - What is the role of the conductor in these situations?
        - What makes these situations challenging?
        - Are there differences between how an experienced and an inexperienced person might handle the situation?
            - What are typical 'pitfalls'/mistakes that a less experienced person might make?

12. Another factor in the job of conductors is working safely – insuring your own safety and that of others
    - Can you talk about some of the challenges associated with insuring your own safety?
        - Can you give me some recent examples?
        - Are there differences between an experienced and an inexperienced person – with respect to being able to insure their own safety?
            - What are typical 'pitfalls'/mistakes that a less experienced person might make?
    - Can you talk about some of the challenges associated with insuring the safety of others?
        - Can you give me some recent examples?
        - Are there differences between an experienced and an inexperienced person – with respect to being able to insure the safety of others?
            - What are typical 'pitfalls'/mistakes that a less experienced person might make?

13. I would like to switch and ask about different kinds of mental demands and how experienced conductors learn to handle them? *[These will be discussed to the extent that they have not been brought up earlier]*

    - One example is high mental workload. Can you talk about situations that require you to do a lot of calculations or mental manipulations in your head?
        - Can you give some examples?
        - Are there differences between how an experienced and an inexperienced person might handle the situation?
            - What are typical 'pitfalls'/mistakes that a less experienced person might make?
    - Another example is high attention demands. Can you talk about situations where you have to attend to or do multiple things at once?
        - Can you give some examples?
        - Are there differences between how an experienced and an inexperienced person might handle the situation?
            - What are typical 'pitfalls'/mistakes that a less experienced person might make?
    - Another example is remaining vigilant when there is low workload, can you talk about situations that require you to keep alert and attentive when there is very little going on?
        - Can you give some examples?
        - Are there differences between how an experienced and an inexperienced person might handle the situation?
            - What are typical 'pitfalls'/mistakes that a less experienced person might make?

- Another example is high memory demands. Can you talk about situations that require you to keep a lot of things in your head, to remember things that are coming up or that you need to do?
    - Can you give some examples?
    - Are there differences between how an experienced and an inexperienced person might handle the situation?
        - What are typical 'pitfalls'/mistakes that a less experienced person might make?

- Are there any other mental challenges associated with the work of conductors, that we haven't covered that you think is important?

    - Can you give me some recent examples?
    - Are there differences between how an experienced and an inexperienced person might handle the situation?
        - What are typical 'pitfalls'/mistakes that a less experienced person might make?

14. Are there other major roles or responsibilities that I haven't mentioned that are mentally challenging?

15. Are there other informal work practices (that go beyond what is covered in formal written policies, rule-books and procedures) that experienced conductors engage in that improve efficiency and safety?

Questions for Peer Instructors and Conductor Training Managers

Opening Question:

Can you tell us a little about your railroad background.

OJT: (45 minutes)

- What do you see as the most important knowledge and skills that New Conductors Need to Learn?
- What types of knowledge and skills do you feel can only be learned on the job?
- What experiences do you try to provide New Conductors so that they can learn these skills?
- In your experience what are the most cognitively challenging aspects of the job of a Conductor?
- What are the things that are hardest for Conductors to learn?
- How much of OJT is rail yard location specific? What are the types of things that need to be learned that are 'territory specific'?
- What are the most challenging 'territory specific' things for Conductors to learn?
- How are Conductor trainees evaluated? At the conclusion of OJT, how do you establish that a conductor has the skills required to work safely and properly?
- In your opinion how long does it typically take to become an 'expert'/seasoned/fully competent and confident conductor?

Cognitively Challenging Aspects of the Job of Conductors: (45 minutes)

I'd like to switch and ask you about the kinds of cognitively challenging situations that can arise during mainline operations and the knowledge, skills and strategies that experienced conductors develop that allow them to handle these types of challenging situations

- One example is high mental workload. Can you talk about situations that require you to do a lot of calculations or mental manipulations in your head?
- Can you give some examples?
- Are there differences between how an experienced and an inexperienced person might handle the situation?
  - What are typical 'pitfalls'/mistakes that a less experienced person might make?
- Another example is high attention demands. Can you talk about situations where you have to attend to or do multiple things at once?
- Can you give some examples?
- Are there differences between how an experienced and an inexperienced person might handle the situation?
  - What are typical 'pitfalls'/mistakes that a less experienced person might make?
  - Another example is remaining vigilant when there is low workload, can you talk about situations that require you to keep alert and attentive when there is very little going on?
- Can you give some examples?
- Are there differences between how an experienced and an inexperienced person might handle the situation?
  - What are typical 'pitfalls'/mistakes that a less experienced person might make?

  - Another example is high memory demands. Can you talk about situations that require you to keep a lot of things in your head, to remember things that are coming up or that you need to do?
- Can you give some examples?

- Are there differences between how an experienced and an inexperienced person might handle the situation?
  - What are typical 'pitfalls'/mistakes that a less experienced person might make?

- Are there any other mental challenges associated with the work of conductors, that we haven't covered that you think is important ?

- Can you give me some recent examples?
  - Are there differences between how an experienced and an inexperienced person might handle them?
  - What are typical 'pitfalls'/mistakes that a less experienced person might make?

- **Conductor Certification (10 minutes)**

A railroad safety advisory committee task force is being convened to develop regulations for certification of railroad conductors.
  - Can you give us your perspective on the need for certifying conductors?
  - What knowledge and skill do you feel is critical for conductors to possess that need to be included in a certification program?
  - Do you feel an apprenticeship (OJT) portion should be included?
  - Have there been incidents that have been attributed to gaps in knowledge or skill of new conductors?

Emerging Technologies and their Impact on Role of Conductors (10)

There are a number of new technologies that are currently under development that are likely to affect the role of conductors. These include new track switching technologies that may reduce the need for conductors to manually switch track position. It also includes new train control technologies (e.g., Positive Train Control technologies) that may alter the cognitive and communication demands on the train crew.

- How do you see these technologies impacting/changing the role of Conductors? Their training requirements?
- In particular how do you see PTC impacting the role of conductors?
  - Handout on PTC
- How do you see PTC impacting requirements for Conductor training requirements?

- Under what train operating conditions do you feel it would be possible to have one person operation? For example are there certain types of train territory where one person operation would be no problem?
- Under what train operating conditions is it critical to have two people in the cab?
- If a railroad went to one person operation what activities would need to be taken over by Loc. Engineer or by an 'aiding systems'?
- What functions that are currently being done by conductors do you feel would no longer be well supported or would need to be done differently?
- What new issues/concerns do you see arising with the introduction of these technologies as they relate to the role of and demands on Conductors?

Questions for Conductors in Mountain Grade Territory

Opening Question:

Can you tell us a little about your railroad background.

Cognitive and Collaborative Demands Associated with Train Handling in Mountainous territory

1. Can you describe some of the added complications that arise in mountainous territory with respect to train handling and the role of the conductor?

2. How do these impact the role of the conductor?

3. One role of conductors relates to being in charge of the train (supervising the safe operation and conduct of the train – managing the train consist and managing the related paper work)
   - Are there some unique complications that arise in mountainous territory that make this task hard (challenging)?
     - Can you give us a recent example that illustrates your point?
   - Are there differences between how an experienced and an inexperienced person might handle the situation?
     - What are typical 'pitfalls'/mistakes that a less experienced person might make that a more experienced person has learned to avoid?

4. Another role of the conductor is to communicate with, support, and serve as a backup to the Locomotive Engineer (alerting him or her) of upcoming speed restrictions, workzones, etc. (and other crew members if applicable).
   - Are there some unique complications that arise in mountainous territory that make this task hard (challenging)?
     - Can you give us a recent example that illustrates your point?
   - Are there differences between how an experienced and an inexperienced person might handle the situation?
     - What are typical 'pitfalls'/mistakes that a less experienced person might make that a more experienced person has learned to avoid?

5. Another role relates to handling non-routine/unanticipated/unplanned for situations
   - Can you give me some examples of some of the kinds of unexpected/unplanned for situations that can arise enroute? (e.g., train malfunction, obstacle on track, hazardous spill)
     - What is the role of the conductor in these situations?
     - What makes these situations challenging?
     - Are there differences between how an experienced and an inexperienced person might handle the situation?
       - What are typical 'pitfalls'/mistakes that a less experienced person might make?

6. Another factor in the job of conductors is working safely – insuring your own safety and that of others
   - Can you talk about some of the challenges associated with insuring your own safety?
     - Can you give me some recent examples?
     - Are there differences between an experienced and an inexperienced person – with respect to being able to insure their own safety?
       - What are typical 'pitfalls'/mistakes that a less experienced person might make?
   - Can you talk about some of the challenges associated with insuring the safety of others?
     - Can you give me some recent examples?
     - Are there differences between an experienced and an inexperienced person – with respect to being able to insure the safety of others?
       - What are typical 'pitfalls'/mistakes that a less experienced person might make?

3. I would like to switch and ask about different kinds of mental demands and how experienced conductors learn to handle them? *[These will be discussed to the extent that they have not been brought up earlier]*

- One example is high mental workload. Can you talk about situations that require you to do a lot of calculations or mental manipulations in your head?
  - Can you give some examples?
  - Are there differences between how an experienced and an inexperienced person might handle the situation?
    - What are typical 'pitfalls'/mistakes that a less experienced person might make?
- Another example is high attention demands. Can you talk about situations where you have to attend to or do multiple things at once?
  - Can you give some examples?
  - Are there differences between how an experienced and an inexperienced person might handle the situation?
    - What are typical 'pitfalls'/mistakes that a less experienced person might make?
  - Another example is remaining vigilant when there is low workload, can you talk about situations that require you to keep alert and attentive when there is very little going on?
    - Can you give some examples?
    - Are there differences between how an experienced and an inexperienced person might handle the situation?
      - What are typical 'pitfalls'/mistakes that a less experienced person might make?

- Another example is high memory demands. Can you talk about situations that require you to keep a lot of things in your head, to remember things that are coming up or that you need to do?
  - Can you give some examples?
  - Are there differences between how an experienced and an inexperienced person might handle the situation?
    - What are typical 'pitfalls'/mistakes that a less experienced person might make?

- Are there any other mental challenges associated with the work of conductors, that we haven't covered that you think is important?

  - Can you give me some recent examples?
  - Are there differences between how an experienced and an inexperienced person might handle the situation?
    - What are typical 'pitfalls'/mistakes that a less experienced person might make?

4. Impact on OJT
- What knowledge and skills can only be learned 'OJT'?
- What are the most challenging 'territory specific' things for Conductors to learn?
- In your view what are some added challenges of mountainous terrain on the training of conductors?
- In your opinion how long does it typically take to become an 'expert'/seasoned/fully competent and confident conductor?

Abbreviations and Acronyms

AAR – American Association of Railroads

BNSF – BNSF Railway

CRM – crew resource management

CTA – cognitive task analysis

EOT – end-of-train device

FRA – Federal Railroad Administration

HOS – hours of service

NARS – National Academy of Railroad Sciences

NPRM – Notice for Proposed Rulemaking

OJT – on-the-job training

RSAC – Rail Safety Advisory Council

RSIA – Rail Safety Improvement Act

TSC – Total Safety Culture

TTCI – Texas Transportation

UP – Union Pacific Railroad

UTU – United Transportation Union